THE ESOTERIC ASPECT OF THE SOCIAL QUESTION

The Individual and Society

RUDOLF STEINER

Four lectures given between
4 February and 9 March 1919

RUDOLF STEINER PRESS
LONDON

Rudolf Steiner Press
51 Queen Caroline Street
London W6 9QL

www.rudolfsteinerpress.com

Published by Rudolf Steiner Press 2001

First published in English as *The Inner Aspect of the Social Question* by Anthroposophical Publishing Co., London 1950
Reprinted 1974

Originally published in German under the title *Der innere Aspekt des sozialen Rätsles, Luziferische Vergangenheit und ahrimanische Zukunft* (volume 193 in the *Rudolf Steiner Gesamtausgabe* or Collected Works) by Rudolf Steiner Verlag, Dornach. This authorized translation is published by kind permission of the Rudolf Steiner Nachlassverwaltung, Dornach

Translated by Pauline Wehrle
Translation © Rudolf Steiner Press 2001

A catalogue record for this book is available from the British Library

ISBN 1 85584 064 2

Cover by Andrew Morgan
Typeset by DP Photosetting, Aylesbury, Bucks.
Printed and bound in Great Britain by Cromwell Press Limited, Trowbridge, Wilts.

Contents

Lecture summaries

Lecture 1

On valuing rightly the human element in the world, and how a deeper understanding of its relation to nature and the cosmos may be kindled in the soul; how the true strength of the spirit is to be sought for.

Lecture 2

Anthroposophists can have an esoteric understanding of the social question as distinct from an exoteric one. Human beings relate to one another in two ways: through karma, connected with previous lives on earth, and in spiritual/cultural life, connected with existence in the spiritual world before birth. The state must include nothing that reaches into the supersensible world in either direction, beyond birth or beyond death. People's connection with the economic sphere must become more and more conscious. Entry into the subhuman realm leads to a compensating human development after death. Totems. Indulgences. A bridge from the spirit in the world to everyday life is needed. Life has to be seen in a real way.

Lecture 3

The membering of the social organism in accordance with the various ways in which human beings are related to the spiritual world. The Mystery of Golgotha as an event for all humankind. Nationalism overcome by Christianity. Spiritual pathways to the Christ: the way of thought and the way of will.

Lecture 4

True and illusory reality in social life. The distinction between a living truth and a living lie needs to be deeply engraved in human souls today. The inner connection between spiritual/cultural life and life before birth. The former should be a reflection of supersensible existence. The political state is just the opposite; its concern should be only with the things that belong to the life between birth and death. In economic life there is an unconscious unfolding of impulses which work on beyond death—seeds of sympathies which are destined to develop in the life after death. Spiritual/cultural life, on the other hand, should be a sort of healing agent for the remains of the antipathies which we bring over from our life before birth into the present. It is only in the diversity of relationships between these three members of the social organism that true reality resides.

Introduction

This volume contains four lectures given by Rudolf Steiner to members of the Anthroposophical Society during February and March of 1919. The lectures constituted a kind of esoteric parallel to the extensive public lectures Steiner was delivering throughout the German-speaking world on the burning social issues of the day. The members to whom he spoke were familiar with his basic esoteric writings, notably *Theosophy* and *An Outline of Esoteric Science.* The reader unfamiliar with these works will find this volume easier to follow if he first acquaints himself with the aforementioned books, which serve as an introduction to Steiner's world view and vocabulary.

These four lectures constitute a small but important fraction of Steiner's social thinking in the aftermath of the Great War, which had come to an end only four months earlier on 11 November 1918. Already in 1917 Steiner formulated his fundamental idea of the threefold social order, namely, the idea that in modern times human society has three distinct activities: the cultural, the political and the economic. He argued that social health would emerge from a proper understanding of the distinction between these three activities and a corresponding division of the social order into three separate spheres that attended to the three activities.

The effort of 1917 was formulated in the *Memorandum* of 1917* after a German aristocrat, Count Lerchenfeld, had asked Steiner for guidance in thinking about the war and of what might be done to bring order out of the chaos. Working with Count Lerchenfeld and Count Polzer-Hoditz, Steiner circulated the *Memorandum* to leading figures in the German and Austrian governments. Probably the most notable development occurred when Prince Maximillian von Baden met Steiner and discussed the contents of the *Memorandum* around 20 January 1918. Von Baden became convinced that middle Europe should be reconstructed on the basis of the threefold idea. As Steiner had anticipated, von Baden was appointed Chancellor of the German Reich by the Kaiser, in September 1918, and was asked to negotiate an armistice.

Von Baden journeyed to Berlin with the intention of putting the threefold social order forward as Germany's plan for its own organization after an armistice, i.e., negotiating this as a condition of an armistice. Before this could happen however, Ludendorff, the leading German general, insisted that an armistice had to take place within 24 hours due to the rapid deterioration of the German army's situation in the field. This left von Baden no time to bring the threefold idea forward. Instead he was forced to negotiate on the basis of Wilson's 14 points which had already been introduced to the world. Immediately after von Baden had accepted an armistice based on the 14 points, Ludendoff

---

*There were two memorandums, which have never been published in English, though this writer has made a translation. The German texts appear in *Aufsätze über die Dreigliederung des sozialen Organismus und zur Zeitlage 1915–1921*, Rudolf Steiner Verlag, Dornach, Switzerland, 1982.

noted that he had been mistaken and that the situation in the field had not really necessitated so hasty an armistice.* By the end of 1918 Steiner recognized that nothing could be accomplished by trying to bring insight to the German leadership. So he shifted his focus to the creation of a grassroots movement for the threefold social order. On 6 March 1919, his 'Appeal to the German People'[†] was circulated to enormous numbers of readers as a newspaper insert. It appeared in most of the major German-speaking cities and attracted international attention.

His book *Towards Social Renewal* was published in April and fast became a best seller in Europe and a few years later in England when a translation appeared.[‡] Writing in the *London Quarterly Review* in 1923 W. F. Lofthouse said of *Towards Social Renewal* that it was 'perhaps the most widely read of all books on politics appearing since the war ...' In that same year the book received a lengthy review in the *New York Times Book Review* (14 January 1923). It was also reviewed in the two leading American economics journals, *The Journal of Political Economy* (1923) and *The American Economic Review* (March 1924). In addition to writing the 'Appeal to the German People' and *Towards Social Renewal*, Steiner lectured continuously in public forums during 1919 and the early 20s on threefold ideas.

*

---

* An interesting historic footnote is that Max von Baden held his position as Prince of Baden as a consequence of the crime against Kaspar Hauser. See further in *Kaspar Hauser* by Peter Tradowsky, Temple Lodge Publishing, 1997.

[†] Reproduced in *Towards Social Renewal* by Rudolf Steiner, Rudolf Steiner Press, 1999.

[‡] First published in English as *The Threefold Commonwealth*, London, 1923.

In addition to followers and supporters, a growing circle of enemies became increasingly aware of Steiner's activity. An article of 15 March 1921, in the National Socialist newspaper *Voelkischen Beobachter*, is the most extraordinary attack in print. Below is an English translation:

It is a plain lie to the German people when, on the order of the German government, one maintains that Simons would have refused. The fact is that Simons had declared himself ready to accept the Treaty of Versailles for five years and, thereby, practically forever. It is straight-on monstrous impudence when this Mr Simons, who is not a reactionary man of God but, on the contrary, an employee of the German people, presumes to announce that the German people cannot correctly value their own capacity for work. It is possible that Simons can actually value it better; the man appears to have exactly valued the capacity for work of the German people. In the course of the London affair there now rises to the surface, by degree, such mysterious accompanying circumstances that it is not only appropriate but also quite necessary to inspect somewhat closer this Mr Minister — the intimate friend of the Gnostic Anthroposophist Rudolf Steiner, himself the adherent of the Threefold Social Order which is one of the many completely Jewish methods of destroying the people's normal state of mind — to see whether his mindless face, mindless according to the opinion of Lloyd George, is really only the result of the lack of spirit or whether it is the larva behind which something else is concealed ...

Poland will occupy Upper Silesia. Germany will rebel.

France rumbles occupation of the Ruhr in the event of German opposition, and then Mr Simons with his mindless, stupid face, as Mr Lloyd George said, will again represent the German people. Then this friend of Germany and of Rudolf Steiner will again make us observe that, in order to keep the Ruhr, we could trade-off Upper Silesia more quickly because Upper Silesia dispatches 43 million tons of coal and the Ruhr 115 million tons. So will he persuade us, a God-and-reason-forsaken people, only yes, in God's heavenly will no real opposition, only peace and prudence, the recognized war cry of the German newspaper Lion and the Levite. We will for the sake of peace, of quiet, and of the Ruhr region renounce Upper Silesia and six months later, due to some other cause, will lose the Ruhr region anyway to the amusement of the whole world. Mr Simons will still have his stupid gaze. As Lloyd George says, he has no mind.

And this is one of the chief reasons for the disarmament of the German people. It is the intention to make the German people defenceless and this does not apply only to the Bavarian militia. And therefore we protest against it and not from a narrow-minded, bird-brained perspective. And what is the driving force behind all this devilishness? The Jews, friends of Dr Rudolf Steiner, who is friend of the mindless Simons.

The author is none other than Adolf Hitler!

Steiner's enemies did not stop at attacks in print. They also made an attempt on his life that was reported as a humorous incident in the *New York Times* on 17 May 1922. Steiner had been booked to lecture at the Four Seasons

Hotel in Munich. This hotel was used, to quote from Reuveni's book *In the Name of the New World Order*, by ' "the mother of National Socialism" the Thule Society', for its gatherings. When Steiner learned of the situation he refused to cancel his talk. H. Buechenbacher took responsibility for Steiner's security.* His account shows the real danger that Steiner faced when the National Socialists turned out the lights and attacked the stage. The account from the *New York Times* follows:

> Munich enjoyed a riotous demonstration when Germany's high priest of Theosophy, Rudolf Steiner, delivered a lecture on 'Vitalization of Thought', before an audience more than half composed of women. Organized reactionaries, Nationalists and anti-Semitics attended the lecture in force, and toward the end the electric lights were switched off and pandemonium broke loose. Lighted firecrackers and stink bombs were thrown at the long-haired Theosophists and then Steiner's foes stormed the stage, and a free-fight ensued until the police cleared the hall.
>
> Then the demonstrators marched to Railroad Station Square with the intention of hauling down the Republican colors. But these are now taken in at dark and secreted in safe places. The chagrined demonstrators therefore contented themselves with singing the imperialistic 'Flag Song' around the flagless flagpoles.

*

---

*'Begegnungen mit Rudolf Steiner 1920–1924', *Mitteilungen aus der Anthroposophischen Arbeit in Deutschland*, Michaelmas 1978.

When Steiner visited a city to address the public on the threefold theme he often took the opportunity to deliver parallel lectures on the theme with more esoteric depth to the members of the Anthroposophical Society in the area, as is the case with the lectures in this volume. A particularly striking theme found in these lectures is the connection Steiner draws between our life in the spiritual world and our cultural, economic and political activity. These ideas constitute part of what might be called the esoteric foundations of the threefold idea.

Another important theme is the overcoming of one-sidedness that has developed in modern times in consequence of the scientific mode of thinking. By its nature abstract and requiring lonely concentration of the individual consciousness, it creates on the one hand the capacity to discover the laws that govern dead nature but on the other hand it dulls our capacity to interact socially. The 'computer nerd' incapable of real human intercourse is a modern archetype of this problem. Steiner gives two exercises for overcoming this tendency. The first is to develop a real interest in the thoughts of others, even if they are completely wrong. The cultivation of such interest creates social awareness that can transform social life. It counteracts the modern tendency to be stuck in one's own point of view.

The second exercise is to create mature enthusiasm for ideals. Young people have a natural capacity to be enthusiastic about ideals. But youthful enthusiasm tends to be replaced by a more cynical attitude in older people. This exercise calls for the creation of a mature enthusiasm that is not extinguished as a person ages and matures. Such enthusiasm has an intentional character and leads naturally to practical deeds towards the realization of ideals. Without such practical idealism nothing of a higher order can occur on the earth in the future.

While delivered over 80 years ago, the ideals found here remain the most far-sighted social thinking humanity has at its disposal. The cultivation of mature enthusiasm for these ideals by a sufficient number of people could still lead to revitalization of civilization in the third millennium.

Stephen E. Usher
New York, March 2001

1.
4 *February 1919*

At the present moment, when it falls to me to give public lectures on the social question here in Zurich,[1] it is perhaps not inappropriate for us on this study group evening to look at the deeper aspect of the social question and work at the significant enigma it has become today.

We know of course that within the outer aspect of a human being — seen from the point of view of our bodily faculties of perception — we must recognize the real person in the inner depths. We first become aware of this inner being when we appreciate that it is fundamentally connected with everything of which we can say is the very heart and core of the world for our knowledge, for our whole life. You have to remember that it is particularly with regard to our conception of the human being that our anthroposophical world view is so different from the ordinary world view. Look at my endeavour to present an outline of the anthroposophical world conception, everything that you have in fact read in my *Outline of Esoteric Science*, and you will see that the evolution of our earth is regarded not only in relation to the human being but as having come from earlier incarnations of our earth planet. Our earth evolution emerged from the Old Moon evolution, this from the Old Sun evolution, and this Sun evolution from the Old Saturn evolution.

However, if you look at all that has been introduced to show the stages this planetary evolution has passed through to become earth evolution you will be able to confirm that wherever you look the human being is there. Humanity is present throughout the whole process. The entire cosmos is regarded in such a way that we see all its forces and all its happenings focused on humankind. The human being is the centre of the conception of the world. In a conversation between Capesius and the initiate in one of my mystery plays I introduced this central focus of the whole of our anthroposophical world conception especially with regard to the effect it has on the aspiring human soul.[2] I wanted to show what an impression it must make on anyone to realize that all the generations of the gods, all the forces of the universe are actually engaged in working at the goal of ultimately producing humankind and placing it at the centre of its creation.

Precisely because this conception is so true I pointed out how very necessary it is to emphasize the need for human modesty and to tell ourselves over and over again that if we could consciously experience our whole being inwardly in its relation to the world around us and bring this, our whole being, to actual manifestation it would be a microcosmic image of the whole remaining world. But how much do we know or experience or manifest in action of all that we are as human beings in the highest sense of the word? So whenever we clearly picture to ourselves the idea of what we are as human beings we always waver between arrogance and modesty. We must certainly not surrender to pride, but neither must we become engulfed in modesty. We would be doing just that if we were not to estimate in the highest possible terms the task we human beings have been given through our very position in the universe. Fundamentally speaking we can never think highly enough of what we ought to be. We can never fully appreciate the deep cosmic dimension of the feeling we should have for our responsibility when we look at the way the whole universe is orientated towards us human beings.

Coming as it does from anthroposophically based spiritual science this should of course be not so much mere theoretical knowledge as a feeling, a feeling of holy awe for what we as human beings ought to be and yet only in the rarest cases manage to be. In fact we ought often to have the feeling when we encounter an individual human being: There you stand; you bring certain things to expression in this present incarnation; but you pass from one life to another, from one incarnation to another, and this gradual process of development bears the imprint of eternity. We could extend and deepen these feelings in many other directions. It is solely by means of this feeling that spiritual science can bring us to a proper appraisal of what a human being is, to a feeling for human dignity in the context of the world. This feeling can fill our whole soul, and only if it extends to every part of our inner being can it put us in the proper mood to sort out, if need be, our individual relationship to another person. We can regard this as one of the first substantial achievements of modern anthroposophically based spiritual science: a proper respect for the human element in the world. This is one thing.

There is another thing too, that we shall arrive at out of an involvement with an anthroposophically based spiritual science that is not merely theoretical but really heartfelt and profound, and it is this: If we contemplate everything that is active in the world in the way of the elements in earth, water and air, everything that shines down to us from the stars and breathes in the wind, everything that speaks to us from the various kingdoms of nature, if we contemplate all this in the light of anthroposophically based spiritual science we find that in one way or another it is connected with the human being. Everything takes on value for us because we can bring it into a certain relation to the human being. Supersensible knowledge leads us to have a feeling relationship between the human being and everything else in the world. The poet Christian Morgenstern[3] put into beautiful verse a feeling I have often spoken about to our friends in connection with a chapter in St John's Gospel, the feeling which comes over us when we think about the different ranks in the kingdoms of nature[4]. We can imagine the plants looking at the lifeless realm of the minerals and in doing so becoming aware that in the order of natural beings they are actually on a higher level than the lifeless mineral realm. However, as the plants look at the mineral realm as the ground out of which they grow they can come to realize that although they are at a higher stage of being they nevertheless grow out of the soil of the earth and owe to it their very existence. Therefore the plant says: I bow in gratitude to what is lower than myself. We ought to have similar feelings about the animals and their attitude to the plants, and again in the human kingdom when in the course of their evolution human beings have reached a higher stage. They must look down with respect and awe to what is in a certain way lower than they — not merely formulating all this intellectually but so that the weaving pulse of life in all things becomes a real cosmic experience of the soul. This is what the true being of anthroposophical spiritual science can bring us to feel. It enables us to attain a living relationship between ourselves as human beings and the whole of the rest of the world.

There is also a third thing. Spiritual science does not talk endlessly, in a pantheistic way, about spirit underlying everything. In fact spiritual science talks not only about real spirit but aims to speak out of this reality of the spirit, out of the very substance of spirit itself. It strives to speak in such a way that everyone for whom spiritual science is a living experience knows that whenever he thinks thoughts of spirit the spirit itself is present in these thoughts. Anyone who is inspired by the spirit of spiritual science — if I may put it this way — does not want merely to utter thoughts about the spirit but to make way for the spirit itself to speak through his thoughts. Spiritual science is a means to finding the direct presence of the spirit, the active power of the spirit.

Look now at the wealth the soul acquires through a living involvement with spiritual science, and compare this with the social demands of which I spoke yesterday[5] — the social demands which live in the consciousness of today's working class. You should realize that the kind of thoughts which form the basis for this consciousness are ideology, a mere web of abstract thoughts. In fact it is considered to be the essential characteristic of all soul and spirit experience that it is merely ideology, and that all that is real are the economic processes. Human beings are immersed in these; they comprise their struggle for existence; and everything human beings think about and know, all their manifestations of artistic creativity, social behaviour, morals and law arise from these like a kind of mist or fog. Everything appertaining to inner life is only ideological shadow images. Compare the inner life of mind that is regarded as unreal shadow images with the kind of spiritual activity that is waiting to enter our life of soul from the direction of anthroposophical spiritual science. The aim of this kind of spiritual science is that the human soul shall assist the spirit itself to become a living reality in the world. This living spirit has been driven out of the kind of contemporary outlook which originated with the middle class and has been taken over to their detriment by the working class. It has been driven out! And what ought to live in human beings as an awareness of the living truth: 'The spirit is in me', now exists merely as ideology.

Secondly, if one relies on one's ordinary bodily senses, how much does one actually see of the qualities of real humanity for the full understanding of which we need to invoke not only Earth evolution but Moon, Sun and Saturn evolution as well? Modern consciousness has no room for the essential human being which, once we have acquired an awareness of it through anthroposophical spiritual science, opens the way for us to have a real feeling for human dignity and value, so that we can relate properly as human individuals to other human individuals. Is it conceivable that in the chaos of today's social life people will find a proper relationship to one another which is essential for any real solution of the social enigma? How can such a just relationship emerge unless it rests on an evaluation of the human being in cosmic terms, which can only arise from spiritual knowledge and spiritual perception?

Thirdly, regarding a relation to outer law people must not turn to abstract conceptions of the kind economists and sociologists deal in today, but look for direct personal contact with the actual facts and events in the surrounding world. With regard to things appertaining to the human environment it is essential we learn to relate to this world. This third point recalls what I have already said, that in our time anthroposophical spiritual science becomes a real soul experience; a feeling for all the creatures and beings outside ourselves, for all that is below us and above us in the hierarchical order of nature and the world of the gods.

So now look at two different things. Look on the one hand at the consciousness of the working class and how far removed it is, in the way of real experience, from a feeling for the living spirit itself and its activity in human beings, how it has reduced all spiritual life to an ideology. Think how far removed is the way a working class person thinks and, which is even more important, feels about his peers and embodies in his general outlook, from a thoroughly radical evaluation of the human being that reaches through to the spirit. And finally, consider how far removed are the almost universal standards of judgement today—with everything being estimated in economic terms—from the kind of appreciation we acquire for things beyond ourselves when we learn to perceive all that may be drawn from spiritual science regarding the relation of human beings to those other realms of existence.

Look at a further contrast. Look at what humankind has come to as a result of the appalling extent to which the materialistic nature of the last few centuries has invaded human souls. On the other hand think of the hopes that can be stirred to life because real spiritual science is available to humankind. Put these two facts side by side and ask yourselves whether a true grasp of the social enigma will not depend on human souls being stirred to the core by what spiritual science has to give. If you have a proper feeling for these two prospects, the hopeless and the hopeful, then anthroposophical activity will become for you what indeed it should become for humankind today: a necessity of life, an essential part of everything we do.

You will tell yourselves that in the whole context of humanity's recent development nothing is more obvious to you than that this social problem should rear its head; but you will also realize that nothing is more obvious than that this social problem makes people helpless to a tragic extent. For at this very time, when the social problem is knocking so loudly and clearly at the threshold of our world view and of our life, human beings are at the same time going through one of their hardest ordeals, the ordeal of having to find their way to the spirit through their own inner resources. There will be no revelations for us today unless we go in search of them out of our own freedom. For since the middle of the fifteenth century we have been living in the age of the consciousness soul, in which everything has to have the light of consciousness shed on it. Is it not a common complaint today to say: a terrible catastrophe has overtaken humankind; why have the gods allowed us to suffer such an appalling disaster? Why did the gods not spare us this, for it is a deplorable situation that human beings have got themselves into? Despite this feeling, do not let us forget that we are living in the age when we have to manifest our inner human freedom, an age in which the gods, in accordance with their primal purpose, will not manifest themselves unless human beings turn towards them and, out of free resolve, take them into their innermost soul. With regard to the most important things in human evolution we have reached a turning point today, and this includes Christianity. Some people nowadays, particularly those who are actively engaged with the social question, have pointed to the fact that we willingly accept Christianity, but only that part of it which harmonizes with our own social ideals. But this most important of all impulses, the impulse which gives everything else on earth its proper meaning, cannot be dealt with in this manner! We must realize that the amount of Christianity that has come to expression among humankind so far is actually only a beginning. It amounts to little more than an acknowledgment of the fact that the Christ was once present in the man Jesus and passed through the Mystery of Golgotha. Two thousand years of the life of Christianity have achieved nothing more than to bring home to human beings that Christ descended to the earth and has established a connection with it. Human understanding was not mature enough for more. Only now, in the fifth post-Atlantean epoch, the epoch of the evolution of the consciousness soul, has humankind become mature enough not merely to understand the fact that the Christ passed through the Mystery of Golgotha but to grasp the actual living content of this Mystery. An understanding of the meaning of the Mystery of Golgotha is only attainable out of the spiritual foundations humanity can acquire now for the first time in the fifth post-Atlantean epoch.

A remark I have often made both here in this group and

elsewhere is that I consider it extremely superficial to say: 'We live in a time of transition.' All times are times of transition! The point is not that one is living in a time of change but what it is that is changing. It is essential to see *what* is undergoing change. I have also referred here from the most diverse viewpoints to the particular changes that human consciousness and human development are undergoing in the widest sense in our time. Today I should like to refer from a particular angle to the changes taking place in human earthly evolution that are occurring specifically in our time.

I said just now that what we are looking for with the help of spiritual science is not only to think thoughts *about* the spirit but to reach the spirit in its reality and to think thoughts in which the spirit itself is alive and actually comes to manifestation. We can also recall the words of Christ Jesus: 'I am with you always, even unto the end of the world.'[6] You are an adherent of spiritual science in the right way if, instead of believing that the entire substance of Christianity is contained once and for all in the Gospels, you recognize that the Christ is in truth always with us, even unto the end of earth days; not present merely as a dead impulse in which one has to believe, but as a living force which will increasingly come to manifestation. And what is this manifestation in our time? It is the substance of modern anthroposophically–based spiritual science. Spiritual science concerns itself not merely with talking about the Christ but with uttering what the Christ wants to say to human beings today, through the medium of human thoughts.

It is like this: In olden times also, in the days when people still lived their lives instinctively, still possessed some atavistic clairvoyance, spirit came to expression in human souls both in their thought life and in their will. The gods did indeed dwell in humanity, and the gods do still dwell in human beings today, but in a different way from olden times. One can put it in the following way. In those ancient times the gods had a certain task with regard to earth evolution; they had set themselves a goal, a divine goal, and this was achieved by inspiring human beings and giving them the gift of imaginations. But—strange as it may seem—these primal aims of the gods are, as far as earth evolution is concerned, now fulfilled. The goal the gods set themselves for the earth was basically achieved in the course of the fourth post-Atlantean epoch. Nowadays, therefore, the spiritual beings of the higher hierarchies (whom in our sense we may also call the gods) relate differently to human souls than the way they previously related. In those times the gods turned to human beings in order to realize their goals on earth with human help. Nowadays human beings must turn to the gods and raise themselves up to them out of the forces of their innermost hearts. They must reach the point where their human ideals, their consciously-conceived aims, can be realized with the help of divine powers. This is the right way for human beings to go about things from the age of the consciousness soul onwards. In earlier times human goals were unconscious, instinctive, because the conscious purpose of the gods was living in human beings. Now human goals themselves must become more and more conscious. Then human ideals will have the power to rise up to the gods, so that these human aims can be striven for with divine powers.

Just think what these words mean! There is a great deal in them. They point to the necessity for human beings, from our particular time onwards, to begin to develop a new, vital, creative drive. We can cultivate this in various fields; above all we must deepen our efforts in the social sphere by looking at the relationship of one person to another in a more spiritual–scientific way. Because in earlier times the gods realized their aims through the human race, human beings were much closer to one another in a way that was appropriate for that stage of earth evolution than they are today. Nowadays people are in a sense being driven apart, and they must look for quite a different relationship to one another. But first of all they have to find their way to dis-covering what they are looking for. This is apparent everywhere at a purely superficial level. People hardly know what it means to be human. Spiritual science, with its cosmic view of human worth and dignity, is only in its very beginnings. In real life a person today knows little about what a human being is. As a general rule people do not penetrate into the depths of a fellow human being's soul. In order to deepen the social structure a new approach to a knowledge of the human being must enter human evolu-tion.

As a consequence of an unspiritual, scientific outlook we see only the human exterior. Therefore it is essential that, in order to arrive at a real spirit-filled social organism, we must recognize that divine activity is at work in our neighbour. We shall not arrive at this realization unless we actually do something about it. One thing we can do is to strive to deepen our own soul life.

There are many ways of doing this. I will mention just

one: a meditative path. From various viewpoints and with various goals in mind we can take a look back over our own life. We can ask ourselves: How has this life of mine unfolded since childhood? But we might also try it the following way: We can look not so much at what we ourselves have enjoyed and experienced but rather at the people who have entered our lives as parents, brothers and sisters, friends, teachers and so on and, in place of ourselves, focus our attention on the inner nature of each of these people. After a while we shall come to realize how little we actually owe to ourselves and how much is due to all that has flowed into us from others.

If we look back at the panorama of our lives in a really honest way our whole relationship to the world will change, and we shall have acquired the kind of feelings and perceptions that are like fertile seeds for a real experience of human nature. If a person looks again and again into his own being and recognizes the contribution which other people, perhaps long dead, or who have ceased to be close to him, have made to his life, his whole involvement with other people will become such that on forming an individual relationship with someone an imagination of the true being of this person will arise within him. This is something that at the moment of evolution we are now entering needs to become an inner, thoroughly soul-stirring social demand. It is in ways such as this that anthroposophical spiritual science must become practical, bringing life blood and creative energy into our social endeavours.

I should like to emphasize another aspect. In earlier times all that belonged to self-knowledge, to introspection, was a much simpler affair than it is today. For nowadays—and not only with regard to certain people's awareness of such factors as property or poverty – a social impulse of a deeply spiritual nature is arising which manifests, for example, in the following way. At the present time we pay scant attention to the fact that throughout life a constant process of maturing is going on. Inwardly honest people such as Goethe were conscious of this process. Even towards the end of his long life he was still eager to learn, for he knew he had not completed the task of becoming fully human. And in looking back at his youth and his prime he regarded all that happened at that time as a preparation for what he was able to experience in old age. People very seldom think this way nowadays, least of all when taking account of people as social beings. No sooner have we reached the age of twenty, and everyone wants to belong to some corporation or other and – in the popular phrase – exercise their democratic judgement. It never occurs to them that there are things in life worth waiting for, because increasing maturity comes with the years. People do not think that way nowadays. This is one of the things we must learn: that all stages of life, not only the first two or three youthful decades, hold treasures in store for human beings.

There is something else we must learn, too. We are aware not only of ourselves but of people of other age groups; and in particular we are conscious of the fact that children enter the world through birth. The consequence of human evolution is that certain things that used to unfold of themselves in human souls are now only attainable by means of extreme effort, either an effort in the direction of supersensible knowledge, or at least in the direction of a real knowledge of life. As is the case with adults in general, it is also the case with children that parts of their own being remain closed to them. This applies not only to the experiences that will come later in life, in the years of maturity and in old age. A great deal that was formerly revealed through atavistic clairvoyance now remains closed to a person who only sees himself. If we look only within ourselves for knowledge there are things that from the cradle to the grave can never be revealed to us. This is also a consequence of the state of consciousness belonging to our age. We can strive for clear insight, yet a great deal in this realm that ought to be illumined by this clear consciousness remains hidden. This is a special characteristic of our time. We enter the world as children bearing a quality which is important for the world, for the social life of humankind, for the understanding of history. But we cannot reach a knowledge of this, not in childhood, nor in maturity nor old age if we do not reach beyond ourselves. But it can be reached in another way. It can be reached if, either as men or women, either in the prime of life or in old age, we look at children with finely tuned spiritual perception, and realize that something is revealed in children themselves which they cannot understand at present, nor will understand throughout their whole lives, if they remain dependent on themselves, but which *can* be understood by another person older than themselves.

It is something which can be manifested *through* the child — not to the child itself nor to the man or woman whom the child will become — but to another person who, at a more advanced age, looks with real love at a young child. I am drawing special attention to this because this sort of present-day feature shows you in the widest possible way that a social impulse is actively at work in our time. Is there not something profoundly social in the circumstance that something beneficial can only enter life if an older person learns from a really young person how to cooperate for the highest of goals? Not merely a cooperation of one person with another, but of the old with the very young?

This social cooperation is called for out of the whole spirit and essence of our time. And when there is an opportunity such as this for anthroposophical spiritual science to be brought to people who are already prepared to a certain extent through acquaintance with its other branches, we can go even more deeply into the social problem. As people marked out by knowledge of anthroposophical spiritual science you have ahead of you a huge task if you let all that fires you in the way of social feeling become the means to be active among present-day humanity.

Kindle a deeper social feeling, a deeper understanding between one person and another when social matters are being discussed, and you will be discharging in a truly social manner one of the living tasks coming into being through anthroposophical spiritual science.

2.

8 February 1919

The public lectures that have just been given were concerned with the social problem, the social demands of the present time.[1] However, our way of considering these has been not only in the form of thoughts responding to observation, but we have looked at these demands as facts, as happenings belonging to the present-day global scene.

It is essential today that these things, which are an integral part of people's lives, should receive the widest possible attention, and anthroposophically inclined people in particular can make an even more profound study of them. For if we consider we are members of the anthroposophical movement we may never forget that it belongs to our innermost feelings to look at everything in such a way that we bring to our observation of the outer phenomena and facts the knowledge we get from the spiritual world. Not until we become capable of thinking of things as having a spiritual content do they acquire their real face, and we realize that although this spiritual part initially remains concealed within the external earthly world, it is nevertheless a living reality.

On the previous occasion I was able to be with you here[2] I gave you a few indications regarding the social impulses at work in human life which also included the viewpoint of anthroposophical spiritual science. We were then already endeavouring to look at the human being as a social being, as a being possessing both social and antisocial instincts. Only we should never allow ourselves to disregard the fact that, as human beings living on this earth, we bring into our earth existence the effects and results of what we experience in the time elapsing between death and a new birth. Each time we return to earthly life we bring with us the consequences of our last spiritual life, of the last time we resided in the purely supersensible world. And we are not looking at our earthly life in its entirety if we do not bear in mind that what we do, and what we experience in the world through coming together with other people, has something about it that results from our life in the spiritual world from which we come at birth, traces of which we bring with us as forces into this world.

This, on the one hand, is what is projected for us human beings from the spiritual into the physical world. On the other hand we cannot allow ourselves to disregard that in the life we experience here on earth things happen to us and around us which do not immediately come fully to consciousness, but of which we take something particularly important with us through the gate of death into the supersensible world which we experience anew on leaving the earthly world behind at death. Certain things happen to us in our earthly life the significance of which does not apply to this earthly life but is rather a preparation for the life after death — if I may use the expression 'life after death' as an antonym to 'life before birth'.

The way of looking at things which I was speaking about in yesterday's public lecture becomes fully clear only when you can shed the kind of light on it that comes from the supersensible world. And this is the direction I want to be working in today to deepen anthroposophically the theme that is such a timely one. Let us look at the social problem as one that affects the whole of humankind. However, to us the whole of humankind is not only the group of souls who come together socially on earth at a particular time but also the sum of all those souls who at the same time are in the supersensible world, are connected by spiritual ties with earthly human beings and belong to what we can call the whole of the human race. Let us look first of all at what we call in an earthly sense our human spiritual/cultural life.

Human spiritual life in an earthly sense is not the life of spiritual beings but what we human beings experience in our social togetherness as spiritual life. Everything covered by science, art and religion belongs here. Also everything connected with schooling and education belongs here. Let us look first at what human beings in their social togetherness experience as the spiritual life of culture. You know from the sort of information I gave yesterday that this spiritual life — everything covering school, education, science, art, literature, etc. — has to form a separate social unit. This can be presented to the outside world only on the basis of reasons they will accept today. It can be perfectly well understood that sound human reason must be totally adequate to understand these things fully. But to see them as they really are is an added bonus to anyone who engages in the anthroposophical way of looking at things. What is called earthly spiritual life appears to someone like this in a very special light.

The effect the middle classes, the intellectuals among the middle classes, have had in the course of recent developments has been to reduce this spiritual cultural life to a mere ideology which the working classes are now making use of as such as their world view, encompassing all the branches I have enumerated, and yet this certainly does not merely arise from out of economic life.

‚ The working class world view today is namely the following: Everything in the nature of religious conviction and dogma, artistic achievement and legal or moral views, is a superstructure, a kind of spiritual vapour arising out of the only true reality, economic reality. Spiritual life is made into an ideology, into something that is merely in the imagination. To those people, however, who are aware of the foundations from which anthroposophical spiritual science springs, the cultural life in which human beings are embedded is in itself a gift from spiritual beings. They see it not as rising up as clouds out of the depths of economic life but as streaming down from the life of the spiritual hierarchies.

This is the radical difference between what comes from the middle class outlook and its heritage, the working class outlook — according to which everything that has been evolving in humanity since the fifteenth, sixteenth centuries is based on the assumption that the spiritual world is ideological, is merely clouds that rise up out of the harmonies and disharmonies of economic life — and the other outlook, the one which has to come, for this alone can supply the remedy to lead us out of our present-day chaos. Here, cultural life is seen to stream down out of the real spiritual life of the world, the spiritual world to which we belong just as much as we belong through our senses and intellect to the physical earthly world.

Having now arrived at the fifth post- Atlantean epoch we
only find our way about in this spiritual life as social beings
in the human social organism because, before birth and
before our descent to earthly existence, we were prepared
for it through our connections with other spiritual beings of
the hierarchies whom we have often mentioned. Spiritual
research reveals this as an important factor of life.

Coming into life through our birth we enter into contact
with people in a twofold way. Let us clearly distinguish this
twofold approach to other people. One of the ways we
relate to others, and we are bound to do this, is through
destiny. We meet one or another person, a greater or
smaller number of people, by way of connections of destiny.
On being born into earthly existence we enter a particular
family. We enter into a karmic connection with our father,
mother, siblings and the wider family. We become involved
in karmic connections with other people as individuals, on
a one-to-one basis. We live out the individual karma we
have with other people. How does this karma arise? How
do these karmic connections arise? They are the result of
previous occurrences taking place in the course of past
earth lives. Take good note of this: When you enter life
through birth the connections of destiny you enter into with
other people on a one-to-one basis depend on the kind of
experiences you had with them in past lives. This is one of
the kinds of relationship you become involved in with other
people—relationships of destiny.

You also have other kinds of relationship with people. In
belonging to a nation you are part of a group of people with
whom you are not karmically connected in the particular
way I have just described. You are born into a particular

part of the earth as well as a nation. In a way this certainly has to do with your karma, but you are thrown together in one social organism with a lot of people to whom you do not karmically belong. In a religious community you may have the same religious aspirations as a number of other people with whom you are certainly not karmically connected. Spiritual life, the earthly sort, obviously produces a great number of social connections among people which are certainly not all destiny-based.

These connections were not all prepared in previous earth lives but in the period of time you live through between death and a new birth. In fact when you approach the second half of the life between death and a new birth you enter into a connection with the beings, particularly the higher hierarchies, in which you are influenced by their forces in a way that welds you together spiritually with various human groups. The spiritual life you experience in the form of religion, art, in national connections such as communities based purely on language, in having had a particular kind of education, all this is prepared in the life before birth, in a different realm from that of purely karmic connections. You bring with you into physical/earthly existence what you have experienced already in the life before birth. Earthly spiritual life, spiritual cultural life, is a mirroring of what you experienced in the life before birth, although the way you experienced these things then was quite different.

Anyone who is able to take a fact of this kind regarding the spiritual world thoroughly seriously in the full sense of the word will be faced with a specific question, namely: How can I do justice in the higher sense to this earthly, spiritual/cultural life now that I know that it is a reflection of what I have already experienced in actual, real spiritual life before birth? I will do it justice only by regarding it not as ideology but as something in which I know the spiritual world lives. We have the right attitude to this earthly spiritual life only when we become aware that in this whole realm we find active forces belonging to the spiritual world. Imagine hypothetically for a moment: Everything thought by the beings who belong to the supersensible world, what they experience as their soul life — whether it is the beings of the higher hierarchies who never take on an earthly body, or whether it is human beings who have not yet been born, who have not yet passed through the gate of birth into earthly life — imagine all this living in a dreamlike reflection in the earthly spiritual world of culture.

We are justified, whenever we encounter something, be it in the realm of art, religion or education, to ask the question: What is living in it? We must not merely be interested in what the people here on earth have been doing, but realize that what lives in them are the forces, thoughts and impulses belonging to the whole soul life of the higher hierarchies. We are not looking at the world in its wholeness if we deny that our earthly spiritual culture is the reflection of the thoughts of spiritual beings who either never incarnate on this earth or are not incarnated at the present time. If we can become sensitive enough to feel such reverence for the spiritual world surrounding us that we recognize it to be what the spiritual beings themselves are giving us and surrounding us with, then we shall be able to be truly grateful for this gift from the supersensible world which we experience as our earthly spiritual realm of culture. The cultural realm is then seen necessarily to be an independent branch of the whole social structure of humanity through the very fact of it being the after-effect of what we experience in the spiritual world before birth. If we illumine social life with the light of spiritual knowledge it becomes an obvious thing to treat this spiritual/cultural life as a separate independent reality.

The second area of the social structure is what we could call the administrative rights state, strictly speaking the political life, the area relating to the ordering of juristic relationships between one person and another, of those things in which everybody should be equal before the law. This is the actual life of the state. And fundamentally speaking the life of the state should be nothing else but this. You can also certainly see in this area, entirely on the basis of sound common sense, why it is necessary that this branch of the social organism, this life of the state, of public law, has to be independent for it relates to the equality of everyone before the law, in fact the equality between one person and another altogether. However, when illumined by insight sharpened by anthroposophical spiritual science we can see something further.

This life, this actual life of the state is the only area within the social organism which has nothing to do with the life before birth or the life after death. This is an area that finds the bearings for all its rulings solely in the world human beings live in between birth and death. The state is true to its own nature only when it does not contain a single element that participates in the supersensible realm, whether in the direction of birth or of death. 'Give unto Caesar what is Caesar's and unto God what is God's'[3] has to be supplemented by the statement: But do not give Caesar what is God's, nor God what is Caesar's. For God will reject it!

These things must be separated as fully as are the systems in our human bodily organism. Everything which the life of the state has the right to include, discuss and agree to relates solely to the interrelationships between one person and another. That is the essential point. People of all times who are deeply religious have always been sensitive to this. The rest of humanity, those who were not profoundly religious, did not even permit these things to be spoken about honestly and sincerely in public. For a particular idea had settled in the minds of the deeply religious ones, namely: As far as humankind is concerned the state encompasses solely those things to do with life between birth and death, things that relate purely to life on earth. It is a bad thing if the area that relates solely to earthly life extends its dominion to things of the supersensible realm, to what lies beyond birth and death. However, the earthly spiritual life does reach beyond birth and death, for it contains the shadow of the soul experiences of supersensible beings. If the life pulsing in the state sphere seizes hold of the life of earthly spirituality, the deeply religious ones called this the power exercised by the unlawful prince of this world. This expression 'the unlawful prince of this world' is a hidden reference to what I have just indicated. This is the reason why, in those circles where there is an interest in mixing together these three branches of the social organism, people are reluctant about or even frown upon mentioning the unlawful prince of this world.

It is a somewhat different matter with regard to what happens to the thinking, perception and soul impulses of people who belong to the economic branch of the social organism. There is something particularly remarkable about this. But anthroposophical spiritual science will have made you used to coming to terms with many a thing that at first sight appears paradoxical.

Today, when we speak of the economic branch of the social organism we must of course fully realize that the way we speak of it is characteristic of the fifth post-Atlantean epoch. These things were quite different in earlier periods of the evolution of humankind. What I have to say in this direction applies especially to the present time and the future. And in this context it has to be said that whereas in earlier ages people's involvement in the economic sphere was of an instinctive kind it now has to become more and more conscious. Just as schoolchildren learn their mathematical tables and other such things, we must in the future learn in a similar way about the things that relate to the economic branch of the social organism. A person must be able to feel himself to be a member of the economic organism. This may well make some people uncomfortable, because of the different kind of habits of thinking and perceiving which have taken hold of them and which will have to be radically changed. If somebody nowadays did not know what 3×9 was, he would be taken for an uneducated person, would he not? In some circles you would even be considered uneducated if you did not know who Raphael or Leonardo were. But generally speaking today, in most places you would not be considered uneducated if you could not give a full description of capital or production, consumerism or the system of credit, let alone that hardly anyone has a clear idea of such things as collateral lending.

These ideas will certainly change under the impact of social reform, and in the future people will more easily come into a position of wanting to become informed about such things. Nowadays one does not know where to begin to find a rational explanation of them. For would it not be the most natural thing to do, in order to find out the ins and outs of capital, to pick up a textbook on economics by a famous economist? Yet nowadays, if you pick up three different textbooks on economics you will find three quite different definitions of what capital actually is. Just imagine what an odd opinion you would have of geometry if you were to pick up three geometry books by three different writers and find in each one of them the theorem of Pythagoras presented in a different way from the way you yourself had understood it. The situation is that today even the authorities in the field of economics can give one remarkably little information about these matters. So you cannot blame the general public at all if they do not look for it. But information will have to be sought and found. Human beings will have to find the bridge leading them especially to this economic structure of the social organism. Each one of us will have to make himself consciously the subject of participation in the economy as part of the social organism. We shall learn to think about how we relate to other people simply through the fact of having to handle all kinds of wares on the economic level, and doing this as a community living in a particular territory.

The kind of thinking you make use of, one comprising the whole relationship of the natural order to humanity, is quite different from the kind used for instance in the sphere of spiritual culture. In the world of spiritual culture you share in what beings of the higher hierarchies think, what you yourself have experienced in your life before birth.

In the thinking you develop as a member of the social economic struggle, what is constantly happening — however paradoxical this must seem to you — is that another person is thinking along with you, a more profound human being within you. The moment you feel yourself to be a member of an economic structure a more profound person is taking part in your thoughts. You become committed to combine external factors of life by means of thought. You have to think out: What will the price of such and such be? How do I obtain this or the other product? Your thoughts jump around over the surface of outer facts; the essence of your thought is not spiritual but belongs to external material things. And precisely because external material things live in your thinking, precisely because you have to experience in *thought* and not merely instinctively like an animal what is taking place in the life of the economy, this is why another more profound person is constantly reflecting within you on these things, and carrying them further in a way only he can do, so that they come through to a conclusion and find their relationship to other things.

And this is the very same person who plays an important part with regard to all that you take with you through death into the supersensible world. Paradoxical as it appears to some people, it is particularly the thoughts we are forced to think about the material things of the world — specifically because they are never finished, never neatly rounded off — that arouse in us a different kind of inner spiritual life which we carry through death into the supersensible life. Thus specifically those perceptions or impulses we acquire in economic life have a stronger connection to our life after death than people imagine. Strange and paradoxical as this may appear today, it is actually the conscious form of what came about in the atavistic ages of human evolution, because it was in those ages that the spiritual world worked into people's instinctive life. I should like to draw your attention to the following.

Among some of the so-called primitive peoples we can discover some astonishing customs. We must not of course think such absurd and stupid things about primitive races as present-day anthropologists do. They think that people such as the Australian aborigines are now at the most primitive stage of humanity, a level at which the present-day civilized races once were. This is nonsense! It is the other way round. What we nowadays call a primitive race is one which has fallen into decadence, which has sunk from another level. Today's primitive peoples have merely preserved customs from earlier ages which are still present among those so-called civilized peoples, but in disguise. So primitive peoples give us the opportunity to study some of the habits that existed in a different form in the age of ancient atavistic clairvoyance.

For instance the following custom used to exist: The members of a tribe divided themselves into smaller groups, and each of these smaller groups had a particular name taken from a plant or animal belonging to that area. The significance attaching to these names was that for example one of these groups which had the name 'rye' — to use the modern term for it — had the task of seeing that rye was properly cultivated and that other members of the tribe who did not bear the name of 'rye' were able to obtain supplies. The duty attaching to the people bearing the name 'rye' was to keep an eye on the cultivation and the distribution of rye. The others, who had other names, took it for granted that they would be supplied with rye by this particular group. Another group had the name 'ox', for instance, and they were responsible for the care of cattle and for supplying the others with cattle and everything attaching to this.

Not only did these groups have the duty to supply the others, but the others were at the same time forbidden to cultivate the particular plant or animal concerned, because it was the right of that one totem, as they called it. This is the economic significance of a totem which, in the area that it governed, was also a Mystery rite. These Mystery cultures did not apply, as people imagine today, merely to higher realms. The counsels of the gods, entrusted to those who belonged to the Mysteries, were the very foundations upon which details of every-day life were regulated. Via the initiates the gods brought order into the tribe through the channel of the totem images, the totem groups, instituting not only the corresponding economic organizations but also bringing to them in a manner suitable for the times a knowledge of the nature of the spiritual world and the part it played in earthly spiritual life.

In the same way as they took care of the life of rights, with its entirely earthly character, they prepared human beings by way of economic life so that when they passed through death they would be able to enter another world in which they would have to form connections which they could only prepare for here on earth through associating with the kingdoms of nature external to man. It was under the guidance of their initiates that these people of olden times learnt to place a proper economic branch into their life as a whole.

Later on this more or less fell into disorder, although it is not too difficult to point to an instinctive threefolding of the social organism as far as the time of Greek civilization, or even as late as medieval culture, especially from the viewpoint I have indicated, and the rudiments of this can be found at least as late as the eighteenth century. Oh dear — a person of today is so lazy in his thinking! People would like to explain everything as superficially as possible. If one were *really* to study the life of past times, not according to what people today call history, which is frequently an acknowledged untruth, but according to how it actually was, we would then clearly see an instinctive threefolding. In the one branch, the spiritual/cultural life, everything emanated from a spiritual centre, which made it distinctly different from the life of the state as such.

When the Catholic Church was at its greatest it certainly was an independent limb of society in itself and organized the rest of earthly spiritual life as a separate department; it founded schools, organized the educational system, even founded the first universities, and kept earthly spiritual life separate, taking care that the life of the state was on no account infiltrated by the unlawful prince of this world. And in the life of the economy, even in later times, there was at least the feeling that if people cultivated brotherliness among themselves in economic life something was being prepared that would continue in the life after death. The idea that brotherliness among human beings is rewarded after death is of course an egoistic misinterpretation of the nobler images that lived in totemism, but at least there was still an awareness of the fact that the existence of mutual brotherliness would continue in a spiritual form in the life after death. Even the excesses in this area must be judged from this point of view.

It lies in human nature to go to excess, but one of the most depraved excesses in this area is certainly the trading in indulgences. Even this, though, arose from an awareness that the sacrifices a person makes here in physical life to the life of the economy have significance for his life after death. Even if it is a caricature of the reality, it arose out of the view, though distorted, of the importance of what we experience in this life in relating to the beings of the other kingdoms of the earth, the minerals, plants and animals. Through becoming involved with these other beings we acquire something that only comes to full fruition in the life after death. Compared to what we are after death, in the here and now we are, as human beings, still related to a lower sphere, to animals, plants and minerals; but it is precisely through having this experience of the realms outside man that we prepare something that is to develop to the human stage after death.

If you look at the thought in this way you will understand more readily that it is absolutely self- explanatory that what we experience through our involvement with animals, plants and minerals manifests on earth as something that brings people together, that surrounds them like a spiritual atmosphere on earth. What human beings experience among themselves founds something between birth and death that is purely etheric. What human beings experience in economic life in the subhuman sphere is raised to the level of earthly humanity only after we have passed through death.

It should be of the greatest possible interest and significance to everyone endeavouring to deepen their lives by means of anthroposophical spiritual science to reach the recognition that this threefold ordering of the social organism is based on the very fact that a human being is similarly a threefold being. As a child growing into the physical world we still bear traces of our pre-birth experiences; we have qualities that belong solely to this life between birth and death; and beneath the veil of ordinary physical life, as it were, we are already preparing what will come into its own in the supersensible realm after death. What appears to be the lowest level of life here, the physical handling of the economy—seemingly lower from our earthly point of view than the life of rights—redresses the balance for us by providing the opportunity for us to gain the time to prepare for life after death. In belonging to the realm of art, religion, learning, and all the other areas of spiritual/cultural life, our souls are drawing on the heritage we bring into physical earthly existence through birth. But through the fact of descending, as it were, into the subhuman level in economic life, into the kind of thinking that does not reach up to such high levels, the balance is redressed in that in our deepest inner being we are preparing what will only ascend to the human level after death.

This may sound paradoxical to a present-day person, because he prefers to regard things from a onesided point of view, and does not want to know that every single thing develops in two directions in life. What is exalted from one aspect is lowly from the other, and vice versa. In real life—I could also say living reality — every single thing has another side to it. A person would know ever so much more about himself and the world if he were aware that everything has its other side. It is uncomfortable sometimes to become fully conscious of this, because it brings certain essential duties with it. For instance, with regard to some things we have to become clever and capable, but we cannot reach this particular measure of capability without unfolding a similar measure of stupidity in another direction. One always requires the other. So even if we meet a person in ordinary life who appears to be stupid, we should never consider him totally stupid without being aware of the fact that in his subconscious there may be deep wisdom hidden away which we cannot see.

We discover reality only when we do justice to these two aspects of existing things. So this is how it is: On the one hand the life of spiritual culture seems to us to be the higher realm; at the same time it is the realm in which we are constantly drawing on and exploiting what we bring into physical existence through our birth. And economic life seems to us to be the lowest of the realms; but it fits this description only because, during our lifetime, it shows us its lowest aspect. It allows us time to develop in our unconscious the spiritual side of economic life which we take with us through death into the supersensible world. This feeling of belonging in brotherliness with other people is the chief thing we have to understand as being the spiritual part of economic life.

Understanding of these things is urgently required if humankind want to escape from certain calamities which have arisen precisely because things like this have not had any attention paid them. Something has built up among the leading intellectual personalities of the ruling classes, as I said the day before yesterday,[4] that does not have the impetus to reach into everyday life. It is of especial importance for a person of today to acquire a right understanding in this regard. You see, the leading intellectual circles of the ruling classes have developed a certain moral outlook, a certain religious outlook. But these people prefer to keep this moral, this religious outlook on a onesidedly idealistic level. It is not meant to have the motive power to reach into everyday life. This works out practically in that you can visit your church every Sunday or even more often: you will hear sermons there, but these sermons will constantly fail to include the most serious duties of our time. You will be preached to about all sorts of things in the way of how to act out of your religious outlook, but none of it has any motivating power. So when you leave church and go back to ordinary everyday life you cannot apply any of what the sermons said about the love of one person for another, and what you ought to be doing, and what you would like to be experiencing of what they have just been preaching about. Where is there any agreement between what the preacher, the moral teacher, tells his students and the actual prevailing mood in everyday life?

Things were different for example in those past times to which the totem cult points back. What happened then was that initiates organized everyday matters according to the decree of the gods. It is an unhealthy situation to be in, that we hear nothing from the pulpits today about how economic life ought to be run. The content of sermons—and I have often used this comparison—is actually similar to speaking to a stove and telling it that its sacred duty is to warm the room, and it should get on with it. But you can give a stove this kind of sermon for a very long time and it will not warm the room! All you need to do instead of preaching is to put kindling and coal in it and set it alight, and the room will get warm. You can cut out all the moral teachings that only tell people what they ought to do for the sake of eternal salvation, or for any other things in the category of faith. You can cut out the sort of preaching that most of today's sermons consist of, but you cannot cut out today's real knowledge about the social organism.

People who want to educate the masses should see it as their duty to build a bridge, also in the practical realm, between the life and movement in the world of spirit and the things happening in everyday life. For God and everything that bears witness to him lives not only in what people dream about when they are floating in the clouds, but in the most trivial details of everyday life. When you pick up the salt cellar at table, or put a spoonful of soup in your mouth, or purchase something for a few pennies from a fellow human being, all these things bear witness to God's world. But if you entertain the belief that there is solid matter, 'reality', everything of a lower nature in the one direction, and in the other direction there is the world of God and everything of a spiritual nature which has to be kept at arm's length from solid matter, because the one is sacred and the other profane, one is worthy and the other unworthy, you are contradicting the whole meaning of a world conception that is real and which is the driving force everywhere, in the most exalted holy realm right down to the sphere of human experience of the most everyday kind.

This is what the stream of religion has missed out on right up until our times when it only beseeches the stove to be warm and frowns upon engaging in real, reliable knowledge of the spirit. If people could only speak frankly and openly about the omission on the part of those people who feel themselves called upon to be leaders in the spiritual life to convey this message, it would be a significant indication in the direction of what has to happen.

In what way do people often speak today about redemption and about grace, things that are the objects of faith? They speak in a way that makes it very easy for the masses: There they are with their believing souls. Christ Jesus died on Golgotha and — the progressive theologians do not believe this any longer nowadays — he rose again. But he did it all for himself, and human beings need do nothing more than believe it. A great many people think this way today, and they regard it as an intrusion into their sphere if anyone thinks differently.

People must learn to think differently! Precisely in this realm a radical about-turn has to happen. At this moment in time there sounds forth to us once again the counsel of Christ, which was also the message of John the Baptist: Change your way of thinking, for the time of crisis is approaching. People have become used to taking it for granted that the spirit is somewhere around looking after them; their religious preachers keep telling them there is this kind of spiritual world of which, however, they give the minimum description. People do not want to make the least effort to know anything about the spiritual world, but only to have belief in it.

It is no longer permissible to act in this way! The time has to start right now in which it is imperative to know: Not only do I think about things—possibly also about super-sensible matters—but I must make way for divine/spiritual forces to be in my thinking and my experiencing. The spirit world must live in me, my very thoughts must be godlike. I must give this divinity the chance to speak through me. Then spiritual life will no longer be merely an ideology. That is the great sin of modern times, that spiritual life is reduced to the impotence of ideology. Theology today has become ideological, for it is not only the working class socialist outlook that is an ideology. It is essential that human beings recover from this ideology. The spiritual world has to become real to them. They have to realize that on the one hand the spiritual world is a real factor living in the one sphere of the social organism in the form of a heritage of the life lived in the spirit world before birth, and that on the other hand a spiritual factor is being prepared while we immerse ourselves in economic life apparently below the human level. As compensation for this immer-sion, the very capacity is being prepared which, in the life we shall enter when we return through death into the spiritual world, shall lead us, if we experience this properly, to a more human, brotherly knowledge here on earth.

What must come about is that we look at life as it is in reality. An adherent of anthroposophical spiritual science will find his right place in the world if he becomes aware that things that have without fail to enter the stream of humankind can become something much more profound for him if anthroposophy is recognized and cultivated as something that is much more than a science, cultivated in fact as something that enters into and transforms all his responses to life, so that he can become a worthy and proper part of what has to start in the present time and which is the only thing that can bring healing for the future of humankind.

These words are a pronouncement of what is essential to humankind but also a pronouncement of what humanity has neglected to do. Only by becoming fearlessly and courageously involved in what has been neglected—and which must of necessity be tackled—can anything of a healing nature be brought about for the present age and the immediate future. This is why, here where we are gathered together privately, I have endeavoured, in addition to what can be said publicly about the social question, to present those things that are the particular contribution of anthroposophical spiritual science, in that we can include the aspects that penetrate into this earthly life from the supersensible realm of eternal life.

One branch only of the social organism, the one related to the organization of outer life by the state, is of a purely earthly nature. The two other branches are bound up with supersensible forces in two different directions. On the one hand a spiritual/cultural life has been allotted us as a spiritual earthly life which—because it is as it were squeezed out of the super-earthly life we passed through before birth—can be experienced as a surplus. And on the other hand, because we are people of flesh and therefore connected with the earthly animals, we must submerge ourselves in the life of plain economy. Yet through the fact that we are not solely people of flesh but in this fleshly body the soul is preparing itself for the following earth life and for the following supersensible life, preparations are also being made in our economic life which, like a kind of springboard, will enable the part of us which is not yet entirely human, namely the part of us which has to work in economic life, to ascend to the human level. We have as it were something in us of a superhuman being in as far as we can enter a social connection that pervades earthly spiritual/cultural life. Part of us is entirely on a purely human level in that we become citizens of the state. Part of us forces us to descend below either of these levels, but at the same time we are recompensed by the supersensible world through the fact that in what appears to our social awareness to be the lowest member of the social organism an element is being prepared that will lead us out of it and reincorporate us in the supersensible domain.

Reality, of course, cannot be grasped on as superficial and simple a level as we would sometimes wish. On the contrary, what it shows us is that human life goes through a great variety of phases of which each phase contributes some new impulse, some new ingredient to human life which can only be acquired in this particular way. Thus we see the way in which the strands of the life we live here between birth and death are intertwined with those strands we bring into play in our life between death and a new birth. And in the whole span of human existence everything fits together with the greatest possible meaning. Furthermore, what we set going here in earthly life between one individual and another, what we do to another human being by bringing him joy or sorrow, enriching his thoughts or impoverishing them, by having various dealings with him—these things prepare our karmic life for our next incarnation.

But we have to distinguish this from what is essential to us for our preparation for the supersensible part of existence we unfold directly after death. Here we are brought into certain social communities. But we have to be extricated from them again, and this happens in that from the very life of the economy something emerges which leads us through the gate of death into the spiritual world so that we do not remain in the same social community we became connected with here but are enabled to be accepted into another one in our next life. This is how meaningfully the karmic strands of our life intertwine with the strands that place us into general world existence.

What we can gain for this threefolding of the social order by combining, with the help of spiritual science, the supersensible element with physical/earthly life, appears to deepen to a significant extent what will have to become the exoteric content concerning the threefold social order. It certainly seems to deepen it considerably, though there is simply no help for it today that for outside people this is difficult to understand. But someone who is in the anthroposophical movement ought always to include alongside everything that has its justification in the earthly realm all those things that connect us with the sphere we enter after death, and from which we came at birth, the sphere in which we find those who departed this world ahead of us and with whom we have a definite relationship. For the finest human achievement arising out of our involvement with anthroposophy will be that it teaches us to penetrate the two great mysteries of earthly life, birth and death, creating a bridge between the sense world and the supersensible world, between the so-called living and the so-called dead, so that what is dead becomes as something alive among us, and we can say of the living: The life that was ours in the supersensible realm before birth and will be ours after our death is nothing else but a different form of existence. Things are dead in the sense world in the same sense that the sense world is dead to us when we are living in the supersensible world. The connection between the things of the world is relative. And when we penetrate these two sides of each and every reality then we shall have reached reality itself.

This is what I wished to bring you as an addition, as an esoteric rounding-off of those problems which it is now so urgently necessary to present to the public, and which those people who are closely connected with the anthroposophical movement should take an active interest in.

Rudolf Steiner gave the following reply to an unrecorded question:
One can actually say of these things: This view of the social organism is a firm foundation. All one has to do is find out how the individual incidences become part of life.

If you know the theorem of Pythagoras you will not ask: How can you justify it in each of its details? If you are acquainted with it you will know that it will always be right where it is applicable, just as 3×10 is 30 wherever you apply it. In other words, you will not need to ask whether it is right or whether it has to be proved. You must understand these things in themselves. So you will also find that with regard to this view of social life you are setting out from a specific basis that simply shows itself to be right; the other things that emerge will find their proper connection to them. The tax system, the system of property, will all follow on in a consistent way. Everything will fall into place if you grasp the living social organism. One result will be that people will not hesitate, for example, to send their children to the independent school. On the contrary, they will *want* to send them, because they will be interested in such a school. And again, in the sphere where each person has a potential relationship to everyone else, in the sphere of the rights life, it is essential to be capable of judgement, and no-one who is incapable of this would be eligible for being voted on to the representative body of the second sphere of the social organism. Things like this of course have to be thoroughly examined. The kind of relationship there is between one person and another, this kind of interest in things, this conscious participation in life, will be there as a matter of course in an independent organism that is on its way to becoming sound.

3.
11 February 1919

A week ago I was saying that we, as people interested in the anthroposophical movement, are capable of grasping more deeply and deepening even further the burning questions which it is essential for humankind to come to grips with today if we are ever to form a judgement on them. We can grasp things more profoundly than is possible among the general public. In a sense we can regard ourselves as a kind of leaven—if I may use the biblical term—and everyone from his own particular situation can endeavour to contribute something from out of a much more deeply motivated feeling towards what our time so urgently needs.

If we recall the keynote of the public lectures we shall see that the essential thing in our present time is to strive for a kind of structural classification within the social organism.[1] I always say 'strive for', for there is no question of wanting to effect a revolutionary change overnight. What we must strive towards is to distinguish between the things that have been affected by the modern trend to centralize. Instead of the unitary state we must work towards having an independent sphere of the social organism embracing all that has to do with spiritual and cultural life and existing autonomously alongside the other spheres of society. This sphere will include education, instruction, art, literature, and also (as I have mentioned already and shall touch on in the public lecture tomorrow) everything concerned with the administration of civil and criminal law. A second sphere of the social organism will, strictly speaking, be what we have been calling the state, and which in modern times people have been loading up with all manner of things, such as state schools for example. This has been the general tendency over the past four hundred years. And today, due to the influence of socialist and social ideas people want to take the life of the economy and weld it into a unity with what is par excellence the political sphere. These two spheres must work their way apart again. We should have, independent of one another, a political state as the second sphere of the social organism; and everything that includes the circulation of commodities, the life of the economy, should form a relatively independent third sphere.

Let us now look at this matter from an aspect not so easily accessible to people who are not within our movement, and let us pursue this to a kind of culmination, so that a deeper understanding of today's human situation may arise out of it. Take a look at what, from our earthly point of view, we call our spiritual life, our intellectual life, our life of culture. This covers everything which in one way or another lifts us out of our solitary egoism and brings us together with other people to form groups. Let us take what for the majority of people is still the most important manifestation of spiritual/cultural life, namely the particular aspect of it which should bring us into a relation with supersensible spiritual life. I mean the practice of religion which takes place in the various religious communities. It is people's soul needs which cause them to seek each other out, and it is these similar soul needs which unite them. Education, too, means that one person cares for another in the realm of the inner life. When I read a book I am also drawn out of my individual egoistic self, for I am not the only person receiving the thoughts of the author; even if the book is read only by some people and not by everybody I am absorbing the same thoughts as a number of other people, which means I have become part of a company of readers who share the same soul content. It is an important characteristic of the life of the mind that this part of our life arises in freedom out of the individual resolve of each single person, yet it draws people together and forms communities out of what they have in common.

For everyone looking for a deeper understanding, this last statement will indicate a connection between any kind of community of this kind and the central happening of the whole of earth evolution, the Mystery of Golgotha. For since the Mystery of Golgotha everything concerned with human fellowship belongs in a sense to the Christ impulse. This is the essential thing—that the Christ impulse does not belong to people singly but when they are together. According to Christ Jesus' way of thinking it is a great mistake to suppose that the solitary individual can establish a direct relation to him. The fundamental thing is that Christ lived, died and rose from the dead for humanity, for what humankind signifies as a whole. Therefore, since the Mystery of Golgotha the Christ event is immediately involved—and we shall return to this point—when any kind of human fellowship develops. Accordingly, anyone who really understands the world will realize that even though earthly spiritual life springs from the most individual source, from personal aptitudes and talents, it becomes involved with the Christ event.

Let us now look first of all at this earthly spiritual/cul-
tural life by itself, that is, at religion, education, art and so
on. These activities draw us into relationships with other
people. Here we have to distinguish between those things
which draw us into connections with other people through
our actual destiny, karma, and those which strictly speaking are not connected with our own individual karma. We
have various relationships with people who come into our
lives; we form new relationships with particular people.
Some of the connections we establish are nothing else than
the effects of relationships formed in earlier lives; others
will have karmic consequences in future lives. There are a
great number of different kinds of relationship between
individual human beings. The connections directly related
to our karma must be distinguished from the wider connections that arise when we come together with people
because we belong to the same religious community, have
had the same education, are both reading the same book or
sharing the same artistic activity, and so on. The people we
meet in these ways are not always related to us karmically
from an earlier life. Certainly there are communities which
point to a common destiny in earlier lives, but with regard
to these large communities I have been speaking about it is
usually not so.

They point back to something else. We are referred to the
end of the period we spent in the supersensible world
between death and a new birth, the time when we are
approaching our next incarnation. Being mature enough
now, we take up spiritual connections with the hierarchies
of the angels, archangels and archai, spiritual connections
with the hierarchies altogether; and further, in the spir-

itual/supersensible world before our birth, we also come close to other human souls due to be incarnated later than ourselves who for various reasons have to wait longer for their incarnations. According to our level of maturity before birth we go through a whole range of supersensible experiences before we are drawn again into earthly life through birth. And the forces we receive at this point guide us to the very place on earth which will enable us to experience those communities of earthly spiritual life I have been speaking about.

What we should focus on here is that our earthly spiritual life – all that we experience by being religious people, through being brought up and educated, through absorbing artistic impressions and so on – is not determined solely by earthly circumstances but by the experiences we have had in supersensible realms before we came down through birth into this earthly spiritual life. Just as an image in a mirror indicates what is being reflected, so does earthly spiritual/ cultural life give an indication of what the human being experienced before entering the physical body. In this regard there is, on earth, nothing that has such a real, living and close relationship to the supersensible world as this earthly spiritual life which, while it shows many irregularities, even these irregularities have a meaningful connection with what we experience – in quite a different way, of course – in the supersensible realm. The fact of our earthly spiritual life being connected with pre-earthly life gives it a special position in life. Nothing else in earthly life is so closely connected with our life before birth as the sphere of our spiritual/cultural life on earth! A spiritual investigator has to draw special attention to this. He separates earthly spiritual life from the other human activities we are subject to here on earth because supersensible observation shows him that this earthly spiritual life has its roots and its driving force in the life before birth. For the spiritual investigator this is what distinguishes earthly spiritual/ cultural life from other human activities.

It is different with what can strictly speaking be called political life, the life of civic rights, the part of life regulated by the state. However hard one may try, with the most exact methods of spiritual science, to discover what this actual life of the state—political rights, civic rights—is connected with, one finds no connection at all between this sphere and a supersensible element. This sphere belongs totally to the earth. We must try and understand exactly what is meant by this. For instance, what is a good example of a down-to-earth, political constitutional matter? Ownership of property. If I am the owner of a plot of land this is solely due to the fact that I have been given the exclusive right, on a political basis, to use this land and can exclude everyone else from doing so. The same applies to everything based on common law. Strictly speaking the life of the state is the sum total of common law, together with the sum total of everything that affords society a certain outer protection. This is earth life proper, and it has to do solely with the needs and drives we have between birth and death. However much the state may sometimes imagine that it is God-given, according to the deeper meaning of all religious creeds the following applies. In the first place we have what Christ Jesus told the people, in the language of that period: 'Give unto Caesar the things that are Caesar's and unto God the things that are God's.' Faced with the pretensions of the

Roman empire he wanted above all to separate everything to do with political life from all that is an image of super-sensible life. But every attempt on the part of the purely earthly sphere of the state to introduce a supersensible element into it—when, for example, the state makes itself virtually responsible for religious life or education, and nobody nowadays doubts that this should be so—then people of a deeper religious nature described this by saying: Wherever an attempt is made to lump together things of a spiritual/supersensible nature with the externalities of the sphere of the state, there the rulership is in the hands of the unlawful prince of this world.

You may realize that however much we ought to cogitate about what the unlawful prince of this world means, we do not get anywhere. Only through spiritual science can you find its meaning. The unlawful prince of this world rules whenever an authority which should be concerned only with the ordering of earthly affairs claims the right not only to govern spiritual/cultural life but, as we shall see later, economic life as well. The lawful prince of this world is at work when the realm of the state includes only those things which arise solely on the basis of those forces that appertain to human life between birth and death. So we have reached a spiritual scientific understanding of the second branch of the social organism. It is the realm orientated towards the needs and drives of human beings between birth and death.

We now come to the third branch of society, to the kind of connections existing in the economic sphere. Just think for a moment of the kind of relation we have to the world through the economic sphere. You will easily understand what this relation is if you make yourselves imagine the possibilitiy of our becoming totally submerged in purely external economic life. If that were to happen, what should we be like? We should be nothing else but thinking animals. What prevents us from this is that apart from economic life we have a life of rights—a political life, a sphere of the state—and a knowledge of the spirit, an earthly spiritual/cultural life. Economic life pushes us more or less down on to a subhuman level. But precisely through being pushed down into the subhuman we can at this level cultivate interests that are fraternal in the true sense of the word. In no other realm than that of economic life is it possible for us to develop so easily and naturally human relationships that are brotherly in the full sense of the word.

Where our spiritual/cultural life is concerned what is the dominating impulse? Fundamentally it is personal interest which, although it is on a soul level, is egoistic. What people want from religion is that it 'saves' their souls; they want education to develop their talents, and they want either to enjoy whatever they choose to indulge in by way of artistic presentations or to gain an increase of life forces. It is always the case that what leads a person to the life of the spiritual sphere is egoism, of a grosser or a more refined sort. This is perfectly understandable.

On the other hand in the life of rights, the political life, we have to do with what makes us equal before the law. We have to do with how one person relates to another. Concern for our rights belongs here. Among animals there are no rights! In this respect also we are even in earthly life raised above the animals. However, both in the connections between people as members of a religious or an educational setting, or as citizens of the state, we recognize the existence of personal claims and wishes. In the economic sphere something can come about, especially when we overcome ourselves, which is not derived from personal desires, namely brotherhood, consideration for other people, living a life that is an example to others.

In the spiritual/cultural sphere we receive what we choose to receive. In the rights sphere we lay claim to things we cannot do without if we want to make sure of a life that is worthy of a human being as an equal among equals. And in the economic sphere something is born which unites people in their feeling life, namely brotherliness. This brotherliness comes about through the connections arising when, for example, we form a relationship on the basis of what each of us possesses , on the basis of what each of us needs, and what each of us has. If we persevere with cultivating brotherliness in the sphere of economics then something emerges from this sphere. This brotherly relationship among people is an essential component of the economic realm if this is to become healthy and sound. And if we cultivate it, it becomes an imponderable that we take with us through the gate of death into the supersensible life after death.

On earth economic life appears to be the lowest of the three spheres, yet precisely from this sphere an impetus arises which works on into the super-earthly realm after death. This is how the third branch of the social organism presents itself in the light of spiritual science. In a sense it drives us into regions below the human level, yet in fact this is a blessing, for from the brotherliness of economic life we carry through the gate of death something which remains with us when we enter the supersensible world. Just as earthly spiritual/cultural life points back like a mirrored image to supersensible spiritual life before birth, economic life with all the influence it has on people – a social interest, a feeling for human community, brotherliness – points forward to supersensible life after death.

Thus we have distinguished the three social spheres in the light of spiritual science: spiritual/cultural life pointing back to supersensible life before birth; political life as such, bound up with the influences affecting us between birth and death; and economic life proper pointing forward to what we shall experience when we have passed through the gate of death.

Just as it is true that as human beings we are at one and the same time earthly and super-earthly beings, bearing within us the fruits of what we have already lived through in the supersensible realm before birth and developing within us the seeds of the experiences we shall have in the life after death; just as besides these two mirrorings of supersensible life we have an area of our life between birth and death that is particularly of the earth, and just as true as it is that our human life has three parts in it, so must the social organism around us be made up of three parts if it is to serve as a foundation for human soul life as a whole. Therefore for those who through spiritual science recognize man's place in the cosmos there are much deeper reasons for understanding that a social organism must have a threefold structure, and that if everything is centralized, if everything is piled on to a chaotically jumbled social arrangement, then human beings are bound to degenerate, as in some respects they have in recent times, which has led to the terrible catastrophe of the past four years.

What human beings shall gradually acquire through working with spiritual science is an awareness that every human relationship is inwardly related to the whole of humanity and to the wider world. This is at the same time the proper way to understand the Christ in our time and in the immediate future. This is the insight we shall receive if we are willing today to listen to the Christ. As I have often stressed, he himself told us: 'I am with you always, even unto the end of the world.' This means that what he has to say to us was not restricted to his days on earth, but he continues to speak to us, and we must continue to listen to him. We should not want only to read the Gospels (though certainly we should want to read them over and over again), but we should listen to the living revelation that springs from his continued presence among us. In the present age his message is to change our way of thinking. As his forerunner, John the Baptist, said: Renew your thinking, so that it will open your eyes to the perception of your threefold human nature, which requires that the social environment you live in on earth shall also have a threefold form.

We are absolutely right in saying: The Christ died and rose again for the whole of humankind, the Mystery of Golgotha is an event that took place for us all. We become aware of this particularly at the present time, where nation rises up against nation in brutal war, and where yet again, when events have come to a crisis, most people show a frenzy of wild rejoicing instead of reflectiveness and an awareness of our common humanity. Do not miss the point! All that we have experienced in the past four and a half years, what we are experiencing now and have still to experience, shows anyone who looks deeply enough that humanity has reached a kind of crisis with regard to a consciousness of the Christ. And this has happened because a true spirit of fellowship, a proper relationship between people, has been lost. It is an absolute necessity that people ask themselves: What is the right way to set about finding the Christ impulse again?

A simple fact will show us that the way is not always found. Before the Christ had brought his impulse into earth evolution through the Mystery of Golgotha, the people among whom Christ Jesus was born considered themselves to be the chosen people, and they believed that the world would be happy only if all the other peoples were to die off and their own stock to spread over the entire face of the earth. In a certain sense that was a well- founded belief, for the God Jehovah had chosen this nation as his people, and Jehovah was regarded as the one and only God. Prior to the Mystery of Golgotha the ancient Hebrew people were justified in having this view because they were the very nation through whom the Christ would come. But when the Mystery of Golgotha had occurred on earth, this way of thinking should have come to an end. After that it was obsolete. The recognition of Jehovah should have been replaced by the Christian way of speaking of individual human beings in the manner Jehovah's people spoke of all the members of one particular nation. Today, however, we are experiencing a great many relapses. What is it other than backsliding when every nation—though it may regard this differently and call it by another name—wants to worship a kind of Jehovah, a special national god of its own?

Certainly people do not speak in the kind of religious formulae they once used, but with a modern way of thinking! They have now become accustomed to using another word for this, although I would have thought the expression 'way of thinking' was a good description. To be better understood we could also make the concession of doing what they do, and using the word 'mentality' in public, instead of the expression 'way of thinking', which I have always used in our circles. So today's mentality leads to each nation wanting to install its own particular national god and to confine itself within a strictly national existence. The inevitable result is that nation rages against nation. We are experiencing a relapse into the old Jehovah religion, with the difference that the Jehovah religion is falling apart into a multiplicity of Jehovah religions. Today we are really confronted with an atavistic reversion to the Old Testament. Over the whole earth humanity is bent on dividing itself into separate sections, contrary to the spirit of Christ Jesus who gave himself, his life and being, for humankind as a whole. Human beings are trying to organize themselves as though they had national gods, as though Jehovah still ruled over them. This was justified before the Mystery of Golgotha, but now it is a retrograde step. We must see this in the proper light: the way of nationalism is nowadays a relapse into the Old Testament. This reversion, which will present modern mankind with terrible trials, has only one remedy: to draw near to the Christ again on a spiritual path.

For those concerned with spiritual science a very deep question is: What is the right way, at this special time, to find Christ Jesus out of the depths of our own hearts, in the way our souls are constituted today? I have often spoken

about this subject in this group from other points of view —
and you can see what a serious question it is from the fact
that many official exponents of Christianity have actually
lost the Christ.[2] There are plenty of well-known parsons,
pastors etc. today who talk about the Christ. The essence of
what they say is that a human being can form a relation to
the Christ through a certain deepening of the inner life, a
certain inner experience. But if you follow up what these
people mean by the Christ you will find that no distinction
is made between this image of Christ and God in general,
the Father God in the sense of the Gospels.

You will agree that Harnack, for example, is a celebrated
theologian who, here in Switzerland too, is emulated by
many people, and who has even had a booklet published on
the nature of Christianity.[3] He says a great deal about the
Christ, but what is there to convince us that what he says
applies to the Christ? Nothing at all, for what he says could
just as well apply to Jehovah! So the whole book on the
nature of Christianity is in reality untrue. It would become
true only if it applied to the ancient Hebrew world and were
translated so that every time the word 'Christ' appears
'Jehovah' were put in its place.

I am telling you the truth, but people of today hardly
have the faintest idea what I am talking about. From
countless pulpits all over the world preachers speak about
the Christ, and because the people hear the word 'Christ'
they believe the preachers actually mean Christ. They never
stop to think that what the preachers are saying will be right
only if the word 'Jehovah' is substituted for 'Christ'.

You know, the most harmful things happening in our
time are caused by a certain kind of untruthfulness. Do not

imagine I am saying this with the intention of offending or blaming anyone. Not at all. I only want to state a fact. Those people who are often in the throes of genuine untruth, in fact of actually telling lies, are ignorant of it, and have thoroughly good intentions in their own way. It is hard today for humanity to arrive at the truth, because what I have called a real untruth has an exceptionally strong backing of tradition. And this intrinsic untruthfulness, which rules the day to an immense extent, breeds that other untruthfulness which has taken hold today in all sorts of aspects of life so that people even begin to ask: Is anything true any more? Is there any truth left? Therefore in those who are striving on the path of spiritual science the serious question arises: How shall I find the true way to the Christ, to the particular divine Being whom we are justified in calling the Christ?

If all that happens is that we are born and from birth to death live on earth with the sort of soul condition that arises when we grow up and develop in a thoroughly conventional way, there will be no motivation to come to the Christ. It does not matter how much spiritual activity goes on in us, we shall not feel it necessary to turn to the Christ. If, without doing a certain thing which I shall tell you about in a moment, we simply lead the sort of life most people do today, we shall have no relation to the Christ.

So how do we form a connection to him? The initiative to follow the path to the Christ, even if this sometimes arises from the dim realm of the subconscious, must come from ourselves. To connect with the kind of divinity we have identified in Jehovah we simply have to be normally healthy. Not to find Jehovah is really to be ill in some way. To be an atheist means to have a kind of illness. If you have developed normally in a thoroughly healthy way you will not be an atheist, because it is ridiculous to believe that the healthy human organism could possibly not have a divine origin. A feeling for '*ex deo nascimur*' is something that a healthy human being takes for granted in the course of social life. If he does not recognize *I am born out of the divine* then he must have some defect that comes to expression in his becoming an atheist. This recognition, however, brings us to a generalized conception of the divine which is not the Christ, although modern pastors, through an intrinsic lie, call this the Christ.

We shall only reach the Christ — I am referring here to the immediate present — if we recognize something beyond a natural state of normal health. For we know that the Mystery of Golgotha was enacted on earth because without it people would not have been able to maintain a condition worthy of human beings without finding the Christ impulse. So we must not only establish our humanity during our lifetime but must establish it anew, if we are to be Christians in the true sense, and draw near to the Christ. We must rediscover our humanity in the following way. We must strive for the mental honesty — pluck up the courage to be able to admit, in utter sincerity, that since the Mystery of Golgotha we are not born free from prejudice where our world of thought is concerned; we are all born with certain prejudices.

As soon as we regard the human being as being perfect from the outset, after the manner of Rousseau or in any other way, we shall not find the Christ at all. This is possible only if we recognize that a human being living after the

Mystery of Golgotha has a defect for which he has to compensate through his own activity in this life. I am born as a prejudiced person, and freedom from prejudice in my thinking is something I have to achieve in the course of life. And how can I achieve it? The one and only way is that instead of taking an interest only in what I myself think, and in what I consider right, I must develop a selfless interest in every opinion I encounter, however wrong *I* consider it to be. The more a person prides himself on his own inflexible opinions and is interested only in these, the further he distances himself at this moment in world evolution from the Christ. The more he develops a social interest in other people's opinions, even though he considers them mistaken, the more he lets these opinions shed light on his own thoughts, the more he is able to look at other people's thoughts, which interest him although he thinks they are mistaken, and gives them the same respect he gives to his own thoughts which he probably considers to be true, the greater the feeling he will have in his inmost soul for words which Christ spoke, and which have to be interpreted today according to the new language of Christ. He said: 'Inasmuch as ye have done it unto one of the least of these my brethren ye have done it unto me.'[4]

The Christ will not stop revealing himself to human beings to the end of earthly time. And this is what he is saying today to those people willing to hear him: In whatever the least of your brethren thinks, you must recognize that I am thinking in him, and that I am feeling with both of you when you bring the others' thoughts into relation to your own, and take a social interest in what is taking place in the other person's soul. Whatever you find when you discover the opinion or world outlook of one of the least of your brethren, you are seeking me.

This is how the Christ is speaking to our life of thought now, for since the beginning of the twentieth century he has been revealing himself to human beings in a new way. Not by inspiring us to speak in the way Harnack does of the God who may equally well be Jehovah, and in fact is. But by inspiring us to know that Christ is the God of all and every human being. But we shall not find him if we remain egoistically within ourselves, content with our own thoughts. We shall find him only by testing our thoughts against other peoples', by extending our interest through a genuine tolerance for every part of human nature, and telling ourselves: I am born a prejudiced person, but if I am reborn from out of everyone else's thoughts with a comprehensive social feeling in my own thoughts, I shall find the Christ impulse within me. If I stop thinking that I myself am the sole source of everything I think, but recognize myself right into my innermost soul as a part of humanity, then I have found one of the paths to the Christ. This is the path which today must be called *the way to the Christ through thinking*. It must become a serious part of our lives to educate ourselves to acquire a sense for considering other peoples' thoughts, and to correct bias in ourselves through conversations with others. For if this were not to become a serious part of our lives, human beings would lose the way to the Christ. This is today's way through thinking.

The other path is by way of the will. Here too, people are to a large extent well set on the path leading *away* from the Christ, not *towards* him. And in this realm, too, we must find the way to the Christ. Young people still have some inborn idealism, but today's adults are apathetic and matter-of-fact. They are proud of their pragmatism, and like to think they are being practical, though it points to a kind of limitation. Present-day humanity has no use for ideals drawn from spiritual sources. Young people still have these ideals. Never was the life of older people so markedly different from the life of the young as it is today. Lack of understanding among people is the chief characteristic of our time.

Yesterday I alluded to the deep gulf which exists between the people of the working and the middle classes.[5] Old and young people, too, how little they understand each other today! This is something we ought to take very seriously indeed. Let us try to understand the idealism of the young. Fine, but efforts are being made nowadays to drive it out of them. The aim is to deprive them of fairytales and legends, and of every kind of education which goes beyond bare, external sense perception and exercises the imagination. Yet it will be no easy matter to drive all the natural youthful enthusiasm out of them. But what actually is it? It is a fine thing, this youthful enthusiasm, a magnificent thing, but it ought not to be sufficient in itself. For after all, it is solely the idealism of '*ex deo nascimur*', that aspect of the divine world which is identical with the Jehovah aspect. And since the Mystery of Golgotha was enacted on earth this must not be the only thing we have. There must be something else besides, a kind of idealism which one has to work for.

Besides the inborn idealism of youth we must see to it that we work, in our human communities, to acquire the kind of idealism that does not spring merely from the blood and youthful enthusiasm, but is acquired out of our own initiative. This sort of idealism—especially if one has worked for it through self-education and it therefore cannot fade away with the passing of youth—is something which opens the way to the Christ, because again it is something acquired during life between birth and death. Feel what a great difference there is between instinctive idealism and the kind you have worked to acquire! If you can feel the tremendous difference between youthful enthusiasm and the kind which springs from taking hold of the life of the spirit, and which can be rekindled afresh again and again because we have made it part of our soul independently of our bodily existence, then you will have reached the second idealism, the idealism of rebirth and not the one implanted in us by nature.

This is the path to the Christ through the *will*. The other one is the path through *thinking*. Do not ask today for abstract ways to the Christ, ask for these real ways. Enquire into the path of thought which consists in acquiring tolerance of mind for the opinions of mankind in general, and developing a social interest in the thoughts of others. If you enquire into the path of the will you will not hear of something abstract but of the need to educate yourself in idealism. And if you cultivate this idealism or, which is particularly necessary, you introduce it into the education of growing children, a sense will awaken for acting out of the spirit; out of this idealism will come impulses to do more than one is pushed into doing from outside.

When our actions spring from this self-taught idealism we are realizing the intentions of Christ, who did not descend from realms beyond the earth in order to achieve merely earthly ends, but came down to earth from higher realms to fulfil a heavenly purpose. We shall only begin to unite with him if we develop idealism in ourselves, so that Christ, who represents heaven on earth, can work in us. The words Paul said about the Christ: 'Not I but the Christ in me', can only be realized by way of self-acquired idealism.[6] Those who refuse to develop this idealism through a rebirth of their moral nature have no choice but to say: Not I but Jehovah in me. But those who acquire the kind which has to be worked for can say: 'Not I but the Christ in me.' These are the two ways through which we can find the Christ. If we pursue them we shall no longer speak the kind of language that is an inherent lie. Then we shall speak of the Christ as the God of our inner rebirth, while Jehovah is the God of our birth.

People today must discover this distinction, for it is this alone which will enable us to have genuine social feelings and open our eyes to real social concerns. Whoever develops active idealism will also have love for humankind. You may preach as many sermons as you like, telling people they ought to love one another; but it is as if you were to preach to a stove. However much you coax it, it will not warm the room, but if you put coal into it it will, and you will not need to go on telling it that its duty is to warm the room. You can preach to people forever about love, love, love, but that is just empty talk.

Make it your aim that people experience a rebirth of idealism, that besides instinctive idealism they have an idealism which they have actively worked for and which lasts for life, then you will set human love alight in people's souls. For to the extent that you develop idealism within yourself you will get beyond egoism to a self-supporting concern for others.

If you follow this twofold path, the way through thinking and the way through the will that I have described to you with regard to the renewal of Christianity, there is one thing you will certainly experience. Out of a thinking which is intrinsically tolerant and interested in the thoughts of others, and out of a will reborn through acquiring idealism, something arises that cannot be called anything else but a heightened feeling of responsibility for everything you do. If you want to see what is changing in your soul, then you will feel, as you progress on these two paths—as distinct from a conventional life in which these paths are not followed—you will feel the subtle changes taking place within yourself as your inner feeling of responsibility increases towards everything you think and do. This sense of responsibility will impel you to say: Can I justify what I am doing or thinking not merely with reference to my immediate circumstances and environment but in the light of my responsibility towards the supersensible, spiritual world? Can I justify it, now that I know that everything I do here on earth will be inscribed in an akashic record of everlasting significance, whose influence will work on and on? Oh! It makes a tremendously strong impression on one, this supersensible responsibility towards all things! If one is on the twofold path to the Christ, this feeling of responsibility works like a constant reminder, as though a being stood behind one looking over one's shoulder telling one all the time: You are not responsible only in the eyes of the world; you are also responsible to divine spiritual realms for all that you think and do.

But this being who looks over our shoulder heightening and clarifying our sense of responsibility and setting us on quite a different path than before is the very one who unfailingly brings us close to the Christ who went through the Mystery of Golgotha. This is what I wanted to speak about today, this path to the Christ—how it may be found, and how it manifests in the being I have just described. For this path to Christ has the closest connection with the deepest social impulses and tasks of our time.

4.

9 March 1919

There is great significance in the way certain people feel compelled today to speak of the human situation—people who are endeavouring, with their feelings and perceptions at least, to see into the heart of social affairs. To point to this significance I would like to start with a few statements from the address Kurt Eisner gave to a gathering of students in Basle shortly before his death.[1] Perhaps some of you have already heard these statements, but they are extraordinarily significant if you want to grasp the symptomatic nature of certain things today. 'I hear, don't I?' (he said, referring to his previous remarks) 'and I see clearly enough that deep down there is a longing in our lives striving to come to expression which recognizes clearly enough that our life as we have to live it today is nothing more than an obvious invention of some evil spirit. Imagine a great thinker living about two thousand years ago and knowing nothing about our time, dreaming of how the world would look in two thousand years. Not with the most vivid imagination would he have been able to think up a world such as the one in which we are condemned to live. In truth, existing conditions are the only utopia in the world, and the substance of our desires, the longing of our spirit, is the deepest and final reality, and everything else is horrible. We are simply confusing dreaming and waking. It is up to us to shake off this ancient dream of our present-day social existence. One glance at the war: Can you imagine anyone with human intelligence devising anything of that kind? If this has not been what we call *reality* then perhaps it was a dream and we are now awakening.' Just think of it, this man—in his efforts to understand the present—was driven to make use of the idea of dreaming, and to ask himself: Is it not much better to call the reality surrounding us today a bad dream than to call it actual reality?

So we have this remarkable case—and think how typical it is—of a thoroughly modern person, someone who felt himself to be a herald of a new age, regarding outer sense reality not altogether as *maya*, as a dream—as for instance the Indian point of view does—but feeling impelled in face of the exceptional events of the present, to raise the question (no matter in what sense, but nevertheless to raise it) whether we are not actually dreaming this reality! Indeed, the whole tenor of Eisner's address shows that he was using more than a turn of phrase when he said that this present reality can be nothing else but something inflicted upon humankind by an evil spirit.

Let us take some of the things to which we have given our minds in the course of our anthroposophical work, especially the fact that in general we endeavour to look at outer sense reality not as the whole of reality but as being connected with supersensible reality, without which it would not be complete. This outlook, however, is no more than a tiny spark in the currents of thought of the present age, which to a large extent is flooded by materialistic thinking— yet we see that a man such as Kurt Eisner, who from his point of view gave this spark no credit (at any rate not during his lifetime), is driven by the facts of his time to the one and only comparison he can make: outer reality, in its present appearance at least, is a dream. Faced with this present-day reality he is forced to make a confession which he can only express in terms of the universal truth of the unreal nature, the *maya* character of outer sense reality on its own.

Let us now go rather more deeply into some of the things we have been considering over the past weeks which have included the social question. Let us observe how the trend of events in recent centuries has brought people more and more to the point of denying the actual spiritual or super-sensible world, and upholding this denial to the greatest possible extent. You may object that in some quarters people talk a lot about the supersensible world. There are still numerous churches, if not always full, which resound, at least, with words that profess to announce the spirit. After all, today and yesterday evening we have been hearing the tolling of bells almost non-stop, and that is supposed to be the expression of what is presented to the world as spiritual life. Yet we experience something else besides this. If right now in the immediate present an endeavour is being made to listen to what the Christ is saying in our present age, then it is precisely the adherents of the old religious communities who make the fiercest attacks on this form of spiritual revelation. Real spiritual life, one that relies not merely on faith or on ancient tradition, but on the direct spiritual findings of the present, is something very, very few people want today.

In the light of this, is it not in actual fact as though modern humanity needs to be pushed, not by an evil cosmic spirit perhaps, but by a *good* cosmic spirit, to think again of the spiritual side of existence, by being doomed to experience sense perceptible reality of such a kind that a really modern person has to say of it that it resembles a dream, and that even a great thinker of two thousand years ago could not have imagined such a scenario as that which appears as outer reality today?

At any rate here is a modern person compelled to form different ideas about reality than the currently popular ones. I know that a large number of our anthroposophical friends have found it rather difficult to understand these particular ideas about actual reality the importance of which I have been stressing today. But you will not be able to cope with life as it is now unless you have the good will to subscribe to difficult ideas such as these. What kind of thoughts do people arrive at today in the following field? They hold a crystal in their hand and think of it as a real object. Then they hold a rose picked from its bush and call that also a real object. They call both of them real objects in the same sense. But are they both real in the same sense? Scientists, whether from their seats of learning, in their laboratories or clinics, all talk about reality in that they call things real only to the extent that they are real in the same sense as a crystal or a picked rose. But is there not a considerable difference, an enormous difference, between these two objects through the fact that over long ages of time the crystal keeps its own form, whereas the rose loses its form and dies a comparatively short time after it has been picked? It does not have the same level of reality as the crystal. And even the rosebush, if it is dug up, does not have the same level of reality as it has when it is in the earth. So we shall after all have to look at the things of the world in a different way from today's way of looking at them from outside. We should not call a rose or a rosebush real. At the most we can speak of reality if we take the whole earth into account, and the rosebush, as well as every flower on it, as a strand of hair growing out of this reality!

You see from this that in external sense reality there can be things which cease to be real in the true sense of the word if they are separated from their foundation. And this means that we have to start searching within what appears to be outer reality—this great illusion—for the true realities. In the study of nature mistakes of this kind are common today. But anyone who makes this kind of mistake, and people have got used to this through centuries of habit, will find it extraordinarily hard to think about social matters in a way that accords with reality. For you see, the great difference between human life and nature is that in nature anything that is no longer fully real, such as the picked rose, soon dies. Something that is not a reality can have the appearance of reality, yet in itself it is a lie. And we can quite well incorporate as a reality in social life something which in itself is no reality. In this case, although it is not bound to die off rapidly, it will gradually turn into a source of agony for humanity. For nothing can prove a blessing which is not first experienced and thought out as a complete reality before it is embedded into the social organism. It is not just a sin against the social order but a sin against truth itself if— and I have often said this—we assume human labour can be a commodity. In outer apparent reality it can be made to seem so, but this illusion of reality will cause suffering in the human social order and set the stage for upheavals and revolutions in the social organism.

To sum up, what people need to incorporate into their way of thinking today is that not everything manifested in the outer appearance of reality, such as we see within certain limits, is bound to be true reality; it may be a living lie. And this distinction between living truths and living lies is something that should be deeply engraved in people's conscious minds today. For the more people there are who take this distinction deeply seriously, and the more people there are in whom the feeling awakens that we must open our eyes to those things which are not living lies but living truths, the sooner will the social organism be restored to health. But for this to occur what has to happen?

It is no easy matter to know whether an external object is actually real or not. Imagine to yourselves a being coming from a planet on which the conditions are different from those on our earth, so that he had never encountered the difference between a rose growing on a bush and a crystal. If you were to present him with both a crystal and a rose he might well believe that the two were equally real. He would then be surprised to find the rose withering so soon, while the crystal remained the same. Here on earth we know about these differences because we have observed these things over a longer period. But we cannot follow everything up as we can with a rose to see in outer reality whether a thing is actually real or not, for in life we are presented with things which require us to create a foundation for our judgement if we are to visualize their true reality. What sort of foundation is this, particularly where social life is concerned?

In the two preceding lectures I told you a few things about this foundation, and today I will add something more.[2] You know from my books the descriptions I have given of the spiritual world—the world a human being experiences between death and a new birth. You know that when we refer to this life in the supersensible, spiritual world we need to be aware of the way in which souls relate to one another, for the human being does not have a body there, and is not subject to the physical laws of this world which we live in between birth and death. So we speak there of the play of force or forces from soul to soul. You can read in my *Theosophy* that in the soul world, in the life between death and a new birth, we have to speak of the forces of sympathy and antipathy active from one soul to another. This activity is of an absolutely inner kind. Through antipathy one soul confronts another, and through sympathy pain is soothed. Harmonies and disharmonies arise between the souls' innermost experiences. This relationship between the innermost experiences of one soul and another is what makes up the actual situation in the supersensible world. What one soul can experience in another in this physical world in the course of physical life is only a reflection of those supersensible happenings— what still remains of them, so to speak.

This reflection, however, must be judged in the right light. We can ask how, with reference to social life, we are to judge what we live through here between birth and death when compared to supersensible life. Having often thought about the necessity of threefolding the social order, our attention is immediately drawn to the middle sphere, which has often been described, the actual political state. People who, in our time, have reflected on this political state have been constantly endeavouring to understand what it is. But you know, present-day people with their materialistic ideas, really have no proper basis on which to consider something of this nature. Furthermore, in recent times all sorts of things have been fused together with the modern state according to the various class interests, so that it is pretty well impossible to tell whether the state is a reality and not a living lie. There is a vast contrast between the outlook of the German philosopher Hegel[3] and the very different outlook which Fritz Mauthner,[4] the writer of a philosophical dictionary, has recently made known. Hegel regards the state more or less as the realization of God on earth. Fritz Mauthner says that the state is a necessary evil, but one that is indispensable, an essential of social life. These are the radically opposed views of two prominent men of recent times.

A great deal that formerly came about instinctively is now being raised into consciousness, and therefore all kinds of people have endeavoured to form ideas of what the state should be like and how it ought to be shaped. These ideas have appeared in every shade of the spectrum. On the one hand there are the ones who fight shy of getting down to the nitty-gritty of it, yet want to give it a form whereby people who have lots of complaints to make get the least chance of saying anything. And then there are others who want to make radical changes to enable people to create a satisfying existence. The question is: How can we actually arrive at a conception of what the state really is?

If you observe impartially what can come into play between one person and another in the context of the state, and compare this with my description of what comes into play between one soul and another in supersensible existence, then and only then do you acquire a perception of the reality of the state, of its potential reality. For the relationship based on the fundamental forces of sympathy and antipathy in the human soul in supersensible existence is of the most inward nature, whereas the kind of relation between one person and another founded in the domain of the political state is of the most external nature; it is based on the law, which is the realm where people confront one another in the most distant manner. If you follow this thought through you arrive at the insight that the state is the exact opposite of supersensible life. And it is truest to its own nature, this state, the more completely it is the opposite of supersensible life, the less it presumes in any way to include in its composition anything that belongs to supersensible life, the more it focuses on mutual human relationships based on the most external matters, those in which everyone is equal — equal in the eyes of the law. We become more and more profoundly convinced of the fact that it is the state's real nature to cover only those areas that belong to our life between birth and death, those that belong to the most external realm of our existence.

If that is the case we have to ask: If the state is an image of supersensible life solely because it represents its opposite, how does the supersensible realm find its way into the rest of our life in the sense world? In the last lecture I spoke of this from another point of view. Today I would like to add that the antipathies which develop in the supersensible world during the period between death and birth leave traces behind which we bring with us through birth into physical existence. These come face to face with everything that lives in so-called spiritual/cultural life. This is what draws people together in religious communities and other common cultural interests, so that they can bring balance into the traces of antipathies which have lingered on from the life before birth. All our spiritual culture should be a realm for itself because it is an echo of our pre-earthly life and, as it were, sends us into the sense world equipped to form a kind of remedy for the left-over antipathies coming from the supersensible world. This is why it is so dreadful when human beings bring about splits in their spiritual/cultural life instead of uniting with one another as ought to happen in spiritual life.

The echoes of the antipathies left over from spiritual life before birth churn about in the depths of the human soul and prevent our goals from coming to realization. For what we should be aiming for is true spiritual harmony, real spiritual collaboration. Where there should be harmony cliques arise. This inclination to sectarianism and schisms is the sign of the remaining antipathies from which all spiritual life arises and for which spiritual/cultural life should really become the cure. We should recognize that spiritual life has an inner connection to our pre-earthly life, is in a way related to supersensible life. We should therefore not be tempted to set up this spiritual/cultural life as anything else than an independent activity outside the jurisdiction of the state, which is not an echo in the same sense but a counter-image of supersensible life. And we shall only really understand the essence of both the state and spiritual/cultural life if we take supersensible life into account as well as the life of the senses. Actual reality requires both of these, for the life of the senses on its own is nothing more than a dream.

Economic life is quite different. In economic life one person works for another. People do this because each one finds it to his advantage. Economic life arises from needs, and consists in the satisfying of needs through working on all those things on the physical plane which can satisfy both the ordinary natural needs of human beings as well as those more delicate needs of the soul which are still of an instinctive kind. In economic life, on an unconscious level, something develops which works on beyond death. The work people do for one another out of the egoistic needs of economic life brings about, beneath the surface, the makings of certain sympathies which we have to develop further during the life after death. In the same way as spiritual/cultural life is a kind of cure for the remains of antipathies which we bring into earthly life from our pre-earthly existence, what is going on beneath the surface of economic life is filled with potential for the development of sympathies that will develop after death. This is another aspect again of the way we can learn from the spiritual world to recognize the need for a threefolding of the social order. No one can of course reach this point of view unless he works at acquiring a spiritual scientific basis for an understanding of the cosmos. But for anyone who does this, it will become more and more obvious that life requires that if the social organism is to be sound it must be divided into these three branches. For when compared together, they each have quite a different relationship to supersensible reality which, as I have said, is the complement to the sense world, and together with it makes up true reality.

But over the past few centuries nobody has spoken about the aspects of outer physical existence that manifest in spiritual/cultural life, the life of the state and economic life. People have gone on churning out old traditions, but they still do not understand them. They have lost the habit of taking a direct way, through an active soul life, into the land of the spirit, in search of the light that is able to illumine physical reality without which our physical reality cannot be properly understood. The leading circles among humanity have of course set the tone for this unspiritual life. This accounts for the deep gulf which has arisen between the social classes, a gulf which can be found at the very foundations of our life today, and which we really should be awake to.

Perhaps I may persist in calling to mind how before July and August 1914 the people who belonged to the leading classes — the former leading classes — were full of praise for the heights which our civilization, as they called it, had finally attained. They spoke of how thought could be conveyed over long distances at lightning speed by the telegraph and telephone systems, and of other fabulous achievements of modern technology which have brought such wonderful progress to civilization and culture. But this life of civilization and culture was based on the very foundations which have produced the frightful catastrophes of today. Prior to July and August 1914 the European statesmen, especially those of Central Europe — and there are documents to prove this — declared times without number: According to the present situation peace in Europe is assured for a long time to come. This is literally what the statesmen of Central Europe, especially, said in their party speeches. I could show you speeches made as late as May 1914 in which it was stated: Our diplomatic measures have achieved the kind of interrelationships between the various states which give us the chance to believe in a lasting peace. That was in May 1914!

But if you saw through the situation at that time you had to speak differently. In lectures I gave in Vienna at the time,[5] which was before the war, I stated what I have often repeated in the course of recent years: We are living in the midst of something which can only be called a cancer of our human social life, a carcinoma of the social order. This carcinoma has now burst, and become what people call the World War.

At that time the remark 'We are living in a carcinoma, in a social tumour' was taken by people to be mere words, because the World War was still to come. They had no idea that they were dancing on a volcano! The reaction is still the same today if you draw their attention to the other volcano which is real enough, and is awaiting us in what is only now taking shape in what people have for a long time been calling the social question. Because people are so fond of being asleep to reality they do not hit on the idea of realizing that within this very reality lie the actual forces which alone can turn it into true reality.

This is why it is so difficult to bring home to present-day people the urgent necessity to work towards a threefolding of the social order, for a division into three branches belongs to a healthy social organism. What is the difference between a way of thinking that comes to expression in this demand for a threefold social order and other ways of thinking? These other ways of thinking actually consist in thinking up what might be the best social world order for us and what we ought to do to arrive at it. Notice what the difference is between this kind of thinking and the kind which is at the foundation of the threefolding of the social organism. The threefold social order does not start by asking: What is the best way of arranging the social organism? On the contrary it starts from reality by asking how we classify human beings themselves so that they take their place in the social order in an unrestricted way and can work together so that the right thing comes about. This way of thinking does not hinge on principles or theories, or social dogmas, but on the nature of the human being. It says: Place people in the environment of a threefold social order and they will themselves say how it should be organized. This way of thinking takes its lead from what is really human and not from abstract theories or abstract social dogmas.

If a human being were to live in isolation he would never develop human speech. Human speech can only arise in a social community. On the same premise a human being does not, by himself, develop a social way of thinking nor have any social perceptions or social instincts. Only in the right community is it possible to bring social life into present-day events.

But a great many things contradict this. Because of the rise of materialism in recent centuries humankind has taken leave of true reality, become alienated from it. In their inner being human beings have become lonely, and most lonely of all are the ones who have been torn from life and are connected with nothing but barren machines, with the factory on the one hand and soulless capitalism on the other. The human soul itself has become barren. But out of this soul void something can struggle to break free from a human being's own individual personality. What can come forth from a person's own individual being are spiritual thoughts, spiritual perceptions of the supersensible world, perceptions which also throw light on the external world of nature. It is precisely when we are really lonely, when we are thrown back entirely on ourselves, that we are in the best frame of mind as an individual to acquire knowledge about our relationships with the world of nature and the world of spirit. What we should be acquiring in the way of social thinking is the opposite of this. Only if we reflect on this can we form a proper judgement of the significant moment in history in which we are now living. It was necessary for humanity to go through this historic moment of loneliness in the course of world evolution so that out of their loneliness of soul people could develop spiritual life. The loneliest of all were the great thinkers who appeared to live in heights of total abstraction, yet in their abstractions they were only seeking the path to the supersensible world.

Human beings of course must not only seek the path to the supersensible world and to nature, but out of their own thoughts they must seek the path leading to social life. However, as social life cannot be developed alone but only through really experiencing other people, the lonely people of our modern age are not exactly best suited to develop social thinking. Just when they came to the point of wanting to attain something worthwhile by means of their inner forces, the results of their efforts turned out to be antisocial, not social thinking at all! People's present-day inclinations and longings are the outcome of spiritual forces arrived at in loneliness and are given a false direction by the over-whelming influence of ahrimanic materialism.

The importance of this fact really strikes you if you ask

yourself something which fills many people today with horror. Suppose you ask them: Whom would you call bolshevists? Lenin,[6] Trotsky,[7] they say. Well, I know of another one—not living in the immediate present though—and he is none other than the German philosopher Johann Gottlieb Fichte.[8] You will have come across quite a lot about Fichte's idealistic and spiritual way of thinking, but this is less likely to have made you aware of the sort of person Fichte was than his well-known views expressed in his booklet on a closed economy, which can be bought very cheaply in the Reclam edition.

Compare the way Fichte thinks of how the social order ought to be arranged for the masses with what Trotsky or Lenin write, and you will discover a remarkable agreement. You will then begin to become distrustful of merely regarding a thing and judging it by external appearances, and will be tempted to ask: What is actually behind this? If you look at it more closely and try to understand what is behind it, you will arrive at the following: You will investigate the distinctive spiritual orientation of the most radical minds of today; you may look into the particular soul characteristics of people such as Trotsky and Lenin, their special way of thinking and forms of thought, and then you ask yourself: How have such people become conceivable? And the answer is: You can imagine them first in a different social setting, and then in ours which, for centuries now, has been developing into what it has become in the light, or more exactly in the darkness, of materialism. Supposing Lenin and Trotsky had been part of a different social order. How might they have turned out, when developing their spiritual forces in quite a different way? As profound mystics! For in a religious atmosphere, what lived in their souls might have developed into the most profound mysticism. You can see what it became under the influence of modern materialism.

If you look into Johann Gottlieb Fichte's *Geschlossener Handelsstaat* you will see that it is the social ideal of a person who really and truly was endeavouring his utmost to tread the highest paths of knowledge, and who developed the kind of thinking that constantly tended towards the supersensible world. However, when he tried to work out for himself a social ideal, even though it came entirely from his heart, we see that the very thing that suits us when we pursue for ourselves the highest ideals of knowledge is a handicap when applied to the kind of social thinking necessary for working in social life. The kind of spiritual work Fichte did requires to be done alone, whereas social thinking has to be worked at in a community of other human beings, where the chief task of the thinker is to consider how the social organism might be laid out so that people may work together in the right way to found a social existence within the social realm itself. This is why I never tell you, or tell the people of today, this is how you should deal with private property with regard to the means of production, or communal property with regard to the means of production, but have to say: Endeavour to work towards dividing the social organism into its three spheres, then what is affected by capital will be managed by the spiritual sphere, and its life of rights will be administered by the political state. Then the sphere of rights and the organizational sphere will dovetail properly into the economic sphere. And the kind of socialization will then occur which, in accordance with certain legal concepts, will see to it that whatever a person earns over and above his needs shall be constantly channeled into the spiritual/cultural system. It returns again to the spiritual/cultural sphere.

Nowadays this arrangement applies only in the realm of intellectual property, where nobody finds it strange. A person cannot keep his intellectual property for his descendants for more than a certain period – thirty years after his death at most – then it becomes public property. We ought to think of this as a possible model for the channeling back of surplus profit into the social organism, even if it is the result of individual effort, and also channeling back what is covered by the capitalist system. The only question is, into which areas? Into that area which can take care of the individual capacities of people, whether spiritual or otherwise; into the spiritual/cultural realm. Things will be managed this way when people take their rightful place in the social organism. This is what this way of thinking will lead to.

I could imagine these things being done differently every century. In such matters no arrangements are valid for all time. But in our era people have got used to judging everything from a materialistic point of view, so nothing is seen any longer in its right light. I have often pointed out that in modern times labour has become a commodity. Ordinary work contracts are based on this; they are based on the amount of work the labourer does for his employer. A healthy relationship cannot arise if the contract is settled in terms of so much labour, for labour must be treated as a rights question, settled by the political state, on the basis of the goods that are produced being divided between those who do the physical work and those who do the intellectual work. The contract can be made solely on the goods produced and not on the relationship of labourer and employer. This is the only way to put the matter on a healthy footing.

But people ask: Where do the social evils associated with capitalism come from? They say they come from the capitalist economic system. But no evils can arise from an economic system. They arise in the first place because we have no real labour laws to protect labour, and secondly because we fail to notice that the way the workers are denied their due share amounts to a living lie. But why are they being deprived? Not because of the economic system but because the social order itself allows the possibility of the individual capacities of the employer to be unjustly rewarded at the expense of the workers. The division of the proceeds ought to be made in terms of goods, for these are the joint products of the intellectual workers and the labourers. But if by virtue of your individual capacities you take something from someone which you have no right to take, what are you doing? You are cheating him, taking advantage of him! You have only to look these circumstances straight in the face to realize that the trouble does not lie in capitalism but in the misuse of intellectual i.e. spiritual capacities. Here you have the connection with the spiritual world. If you start by making the spiritual organization healthy, so that spiritual, intellectual capacities are no longer permitted to take advantage of those who have to labour, then you will be bringing health into the social organism as a whole. It all depends on being able to see what is the right thing to do in every case.

To do this human beings need guiding principles. Today we have reached the point in time when proper guiding principles can only come from spiritual life. Therefore we have to give our serious attention to this spiritual life. And it has to be pointed out again and again that nowadays it is not enough to keep on declaring: People must recapture a belief in the spirit. Oh, plenty of prophets are beginning to speak of the necessity of believing in the spirit! But the point is not merely to say: In order to be cured of the present unhealthy conditions people will have to turn from materialism back to the spirit. No, mere belief in the spirit is no cure for today. However many illustrious prophets go round repeating: People must become spiritual. However many prophets say: Up to now the Christ has only been the concern of our private life, now he should enter the life of the state. Saying things of this sort achieves absolutely nothing today. For what matters now is not merely to believe in the spirit but to be filled with the spirit to the point where we shall be the very people who will bring the spirit into outer material reality. The essential thing today is not to tell people to believe in the spirit, but to speak of the kind of spirit which is really able to master material reality, which is really able to tell us how we should organize the social organism. For the cause of the unspiritual character of the present day is not that human beings do not believe in the spirit but that they cannot enter into the kind of connection with the spirit that would enable the spirit to seize hold of the matter of real life.

Lack of faith in the spirit does not come solely from denying the spirit, it can also come from the assumption that matter is unspiritual. How many people are there today who imagine they are highly superior when they say: Oh! look how unspiritual outer material existence is; we ought to withdraw from it; we must turn away from external material life to the secluded life of the spirit. Down here is material reality, where you use the coupons in your ration book, then you sit down to meditate, and off you go to the spiritual world. Two beautifully distinct ways of living, sharply distinguished!

But this is not what it is all about. The essential thing is that the spirit should become so strong in people's innermost souls that it does not merely aspire to talk about things such as grace and salvation but enters right into what we have to do in outer material reality, that we enable the spirit to flow into this external material reality. To acquire the habit of talking about the spirit comes very easily to people, and in this connection some people can contradict themselves in an extraordinary way. Anzengruber's dramatic personification of the human being who denies God is an illustration of this.[9] Special emphasis is given to the denial by using the words: 'As truly as there is a God in heaven I am an atheist.' There are inconsistent people around today in no small numbers even though they may not draw attention to themselves in such a striking way. But it is a common style today to use expressions such as: As truly as there is a God in heaven I am an atheist!

This sort of thing most certainly conveys a warning not to think that mere belief in the spirit is enough but to try more than anything else to find the spirit in a way that will make us strong enough also to penetrate into outer material reality. Then people will really stop using the word spirit, spirit, spirit in every sentence and show instead, by the way they regard things, that they bring spirit into their observation. The essential thing today is that we look at things in the light of the spirit, and not only talk about spirit. People need to understand this, so that anthroposophical spiritual science is in no way confused with all the superficial talk about spirit which is so popular nowadays. Again and again, when some Sunday afternoon preacher of the worldly sort has merely spoken in a better style than usual, you hear someone saying that it sounds just like anthroposophy. In fact it is usually the opposite! This is precisely what we have to keep a wakeful eye on. This is what it is all about.

If you understand this then you will be very close to the insight that such a well-intentioned statement—I might say a statement spoken out of a presentiment of tragic death—as the one I quoted from Kurt Eisner, is particularly valuable because it strikes one as being someone's confession: 'To be honest, I don't seriously believe in a supersensible element, at least I have no wish to give it any active attention. Yet those who speak about the world of the supersensible have always said: The reality we perceive here with our senses is only the half of reality, it is like a dream! I have only to look at the form this sense reality has taken on in the social life of today, and it does indeed look very like a dream! The fact is, one is driven to say that this reality is clearly the invention of some evil spirit.'

Certainly a remarkable confession! But might it not signify something else? Might not this terrible and tragic manner in which present-day reality is being presented to us be an educative gesture of a good spirit, urging us to seek true reality in what appears as a frightful nightmare, to seek the wholeness of reality, which is compounded of the sense perceptible dimension and the supersensible dimension? We must not take an exclusively pessimistic view of the present time; we can also draw from it the strength to achieve a kind of vindication of contemporary existence. In which case we should never again allow ourselves to stop short at the level of the sense-perceptible but will have to find the way out of it to the supersensible level. For anyone who refuses to seek this way out would have to be pretty dim-witted not to say: This kind of reality is the invention of an evil spirit! But anyone who musters the will to rise from this kind of reality to spiritual reality will also be able to speak in terms of our being taught by a good spirit. And despite all that we see today, we may nevertheless rest assured that humankind will find their way out of the tragic destiny of the present time. But we must of course respond to the clear pointer calling us to play our part in social healing. I wanted to add this today to what I said recently.

Notes

Lecture 1 (pages 1–16)

1. The four public lectures in Zurich were given on 3, 5, 10 and 12 February 1919, published in *Die Soziale Frage*, Dornach 1977.
2. 'The Soul's Probation', Scene 1.
3. Christian Morgenstern (1871–1914) in *Wir fanden einen Pfad*, in the poem 'Die Fusswaschung' (The washing of the feet).
4. John 13, 1–12.
5. On 3 February 1919, see Note 1.
6. Matthew 28, 20.

Lecture 2 (pages 17–43)

1. Lectures given in Berne on 6 February 1919 and in Zurich on 7 February.
2. R. Steiner *Social and Anti-social Forces in the Human Being*, Mercury Press, New York 1982, lecture of 12 December 1918.
3. Luke 20, 25 (*inter alia*).
4. Lecture of 6 February 1919.

Lecture 3 (pages 44–66)

1. See Note 1 to Lecture 1.
2. R. Steiner *The Work of the Angels in Man's Astral Body*, Rudolf Steiner Press 1972, lecture of 9 October 1918; *Evil*, Rudolf Steiner Press, London 1977, lecture of 16 October 1918.
3. Adolf von Harnack (1851–1930). Professor of Theology in

Berlin. *Das Wesen des Christentums* (The essence of Christianity), Leipzig 1900.
4. Matthew 25, 40.
5. Lecture of 10 February 1919. See Note 1 to Lecture 1.
6. Galatians 2, 20.

Lecture 4 (pages 67–89)

1. Kurt Eisner (1867–1919). Socialist politician and premier of Bavaria. Assassinated 1919. Lecture to students on 10 February 1919 entitled 'Der Sozialismus und die Jugend' (Socialism and Youth).
2. First and third lectures in this volume.
3. Georg Friedrich Wilhelm Hegel (1770–1831). *The Philosophy of Right* (written 1820, English 1896 by S. W. Dyde).
4. Fritz Mauthner (1849–1923). *Beiträge zu einer Kritik der Sprache*, 1901–02.
5. R. Steiner *The Inner Nature of Man* (GA 153), Rudolf Steiner Press, London 1994.
6. Vladimir Ilich Ulyanov (1870–1924).
7. Leo Davidovich Trotsky (1879–1940).
8. Johann Gottlieb Fichte (1762–1814), *Der geschlossene Handelsstaat* (The exclusive or isolated commercial state), written 1800.
9. Ludwig Anzengruber (1839–1889). Austrian writer.

Publisher's note regarding Rudolf Steiner's lectures

The lectures and addresses contained in this volume have been translated from the German, which is based on stenographic and other recorded texts that were in most cases never seen or revised by the lecturer. Hence, due to human errors in hearing and transcription, they may contain mistakes and faulty passages. Every effort has been made to ensure that this is not the case. Some of the lectures were given to audiences more familiar with anthroposophy; these are the so-called 'private' or 'members' lectures. Other lectures, like the written works, were intended for the general public. The difference between these, as Rudolf Steiner indicates in his *Autobiography*, is twofold. On the one hand, the lectures given to members of the Anthroposophical Society take for granted a background in and commitment to anthroposophy; in the public lectures this was not the case. At the same time, the members' lectures address the concerns and dilemmas of the members, while the public work speaks directly out of Steiner's own understanding of universal needs. Nevertheless, as Rudolf Steiner stresses: 'Nothing was ever said that was not solely the result of my direct experience of the growing content of anthroposophy. There was never any question of concessions to the prejudices and preferences of the members. Whoever reads these privately printed lectures can take them to represent anthroposophy in the fullest sense. Thus it was possible without hesitation—when the complaints in this direction became too persistent — to depart from the custom of circulating this material "For members only". But it must be borne in mind that faulty passages do occur in these reports not revised by myself.' Earlier in the same chapter, he states: 'Had I been able to correct them [the private lectures], the restriction *for members only* would have been unnecessary from the beginning.'

TOWARDS SOCIAL RENEWAL
Rethinking the Basis of Society
Rudolf Steiner

Although this book was first published in 1919, it remains highly relevant to social problems encountered today. Uniquely, Steiner's social thinking is not based on intellectual theory, but on a profound perception of the archetypal spiritual nature of social life. As he suggests in this classic work, society has three distinct realms—the economic, the political (individual human rights), and the cultural (spiritual). While social life as a whole is a unity, the autonomy of these three sectors should be respected if our increasing social problems are to be resolved.

Steiner relates the ideals of 'liberty, equality and fraternity' to modern society. Economics calls for *fraternity*, political rights require *equality*, while culture should be characterised by *liberty* (freedom). The slogans of the French Revolution, he suggests, can only become truly manifest if our social thinking is transformed to correspond to the spiritual reality.

144pp; £9.95; ISBN 1-85584-072-3